FLASHBACKS

ON RETURNING TO VIETNAM

Morley Safer

RANDOM HOUSE 🏠 NEW YORK

Grateful acknowledgment is made to Almo Music Corporation for permission
to reprint an excerpt from the song "Top of the World," lyrics by John Bettis,
music by Richard Carpenter. Copyright © 1972 by Almo Music Corporation
and Hammer and Nails Music (ASCAP). All rights reserved.
International copyright secured. Reprinted by permission.

Library of Congress Cataloging-in-Publication Data

Safer, Morley.
Flashbacks: on returning to Vietnam / Morley Safer.
p.   cm.
ISBN 0-394-58374-4
1. Vietnam—Description and travel—1975- 2. Vietnamese Conflict,
1961-1975—Personal narratives, American. 3. Safer, Morley—
Journeys—Vietnam. I. Title.
DS556.39.S24   1990
959.704'38—dc20   89-24242

Manufactured in the United States of America

2 4 6 8 9 7 5 3

FIRST EDITION

Book design by Carole Lowenstein

FLASHBACKS

To Pop

Earth has waited for them,
All the time of their growth
Fretting for their decay:
Now she has them at last!
In the strength of their strength
Suspended—stopped and held.

"Dead Man's Dump"
ISAAC ROSENBERG 1890–1915

Acknowledgments

Thanks are especially due to Fred Friendly, my first boss at CBS News, to Dick Salant, Bill Leonard, Howard Stringer, and the current administration, which has had to deal with not only the external batterings of outraged government and industry but with internal alarms and insurrections as well. To Walter Cronkite, who a quarter of a century ago placed his considerable reputation on the line in defending his reporters' right to report bad news . . . and of course to Don Hewitt, the manic genius who created *60 Minutes* and whose balmy idea enhanced so many people's lives. All of them men of good spirit and goodwill, who, in ways they may not even know, contributed to this book. I ask for forgiveness for the few slings I toss their way.

Joe Peyronnin, the vice president of CBS News, did not hesitate in offering his help in gaining access to CBS photographic material. Patti Hassler not only gave me continuous encouragement in this enterprise, she filled in the blanks of a fading memory. My assistant,

Lee Solomon, demonstrated resourcefulness and enthusiasm that is infectious. Kathleen Ryan tried valiantly to unravel for me the mysteries of word processing. Her hard work made the manuscript legible. Mimi Edmunds, Paul Oppenheim, and Wade Bingham were members of the caravan without whom the caravan would have been a stationary one. Allan Wegman in New York was always there when I needed his help. David Butler in Bangkok gave me perceptive guidance in person, on the telephone, and in his excellent book *The Fall of Saigon.*

I thank Ha Thuc Can in Singapore for a thousand kindnesses over the years, and John and Wendy Tiffin in London for their support and friendship in everything I have ever undertaken. Peter Osnos of Random House made the publication of this book not only possible but at times even pleasurable. Ronald Konecky defies the wisdom that you can't be friends with your lawyer.

Jane and Sarah Safer gave their love and understanding and above all their patience.

And most of all I want to thank Harry Reasoner. Had it not been for his generosity, the journey back to Vietnam would not have been taken.

Acknowledgments

Contents

Contents

Introduction

Not until I returned to Vietnam in January of 1989 did I really begin to understand the grip the place had maintained on me. As I typed the day's notes the first night in Hanoi I found myself rambling back twenty-five years to when I first arrived in the country. What I was writing bore little relevance to the story I had come back to report. It was something like rummaging through an attic seeking a specific shoebox and being ambushed by the commandos of nostalgia.

"The leaves of memory," Longfellow wrote, "seemed to make a mournful rustling in the dark."

The notes became a letter to my daughter Sarah. The letter became this book.

Vietnam entered my life just after Christmas 1964, when I received a call in London from Ralph Paskman, the manager of CBS News in New York. Ralph was not a man to dwell on the niceties. There was no well-wishing for the new year. He went straight to the point.

"I want you to go to Saigon," he said.

"For how long?"

"As long as there are stories. Three months maybe. Six at the most. American troops will be out in six months."

I had little interest in Southeast Asia. As a London correspondent for the previous five years I had covered the various alarms in the Middle East and Africa, covering British and European politics during tamer intervals.

Over the next few weeks I read the clipping files and a number of books on the French colonial war against the Viet Minh, the forerunner of the Vietcong.

Nothing prepared me for what I found in Saigon. Both the physical and psychological terrain was being prepared for a colossal American intervention. Machismo was in the air. American military advisers—there were no full-scale units—were beginning to strut their stuff. They were giving up their role of bystanders and sideline coaches. The war was ceasing to be a Vietnamese show.

Paskman's three-to-six-month war lasted another decade. Three million Americans fought in it. Almost sixty thousand were killed and three hundred thousand wounded. The North and South Vietnamese lost between a million and a half and two million men and women, and no estimate has even been made of the numbers of their wounded. Statistics were not a major concern of either Vietnamese nation. The United States was obsessed with them.

The commitment made by American publishers and networks to covering the war matched that of three presidents to winning it. The total effect of the Vietnam War on American society is still being calculated. One effect, certainly, was to change—possibly forever—the way in which war is reported and the way reporters are perceived.

I stayed in Vietnam through most of 1965, returned in 1966 for most of another year, and went back again in 1970 and 1971.

When I returned yet again last year, I was, as on my prior visits, not prepared for what I found.

I expected the Vietnamese to be embittered. Instead I found a nation trying to get on with its life, a society still digging out from the rubble of war and its melancholy aftereffects.

The new, unified Vietnam is a nation formed of two economic disaster areas, both crippled by the grotesque tinkering of theorists. Probably the only salvation for the country is, ironically, the intervention of the United States. Vietnam is desperate for what it calls reconciliation, which translates as American aid. Beyond the obvious self-interest there is a genuine affection that the Vietnamese feel toward Americans. They are acutely aware of the generosity and compassion instinctive in the people who tried so hard to kill them less than a generation ago.

The veterans I met are all extremely patriotic men and women, but none of them, with the possible exception of General Giap, could be described as war lovers. Such a person in Vietnam would, I suspect, be shunned as boastful and foolish. The young people regard the war merely as history. The blood of their families and enemies has become so much dust to stalk the bookshelves and clog the mind.

I acknowledge a great affection and admiration for the Vietnamese people, for that special mixture of stoic acceptance of life as it is while maintaining faith that there are always wonderful possibilities. The one constant in their rotten history is their "Vietnameseness," which I can only translate as endurance.

The journal that follows, like all traveler's tales, like all memories of war, is extremely personal, unbound by the constraints of journalistic objectivity.

Each witness to Vietnam has his own set of "flashbacks," his own scrapbook of conflicting verities. As different as each is, they all seem to point to the same conclusion: We are all still imprisoned, to one extent or another, by that place and that time.

FLASHBACKS

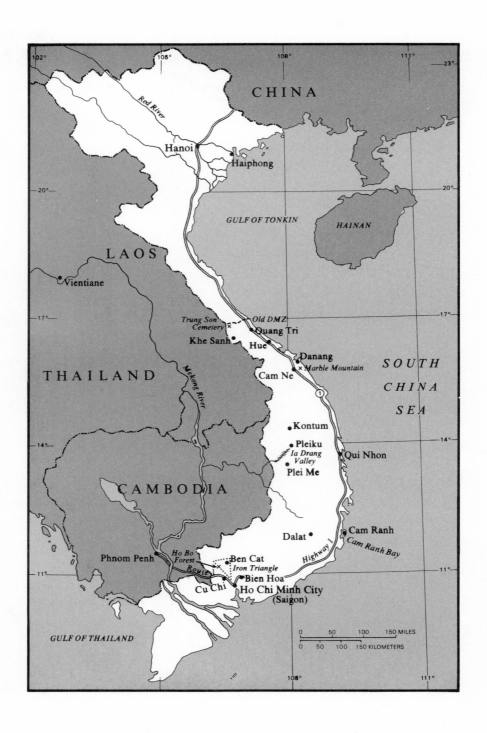

CHINA

Red River

Hanoi

Haiphong

GULF OF TONKIN

HAINAN

LAOS

Vientiane

THAILAND

Mekong River

Trung Son
Cemetery

Old DMZ

Quang Tri

Khe Sanh

Hue

Danang

× Marble Mountain

Cam Ne

SOUTH
CHINA
SEA

1

Kontum

Pleiku

Ia Drang
Valley

Qui Nhon

Plei Me

CAMBODIA

Dalat

Cam Ranh

Cam Ranh Bay

Phnom Penh

Ho Bo
Forest

Route

Ben Cat

Iron Triangle

Highway 1

Cu Chi

Bien Hoa

Ho Chi Minh City
(Saigon)

GULF OF THAILAND

| 0 | 50 | 100 | 150 MILES |

| 0 | 50 | 100 | 150 KILOMETERS |

1

Arrival

Hanoi, January 18, 4:00 P.M.: It is definitely not a bomber's day as the Thai Airways flight arrives over Hanoi. The ceiling is something under one thousand feet, and the plane is bouncing badly. For a moment I think there is no way we can land here and that we will turn back to Bangkok. But the pilot has obviously done this before, come through the mucky skies of a Hanoi winter. All hundred and nineteen passengers applaud when he lands hard, very hard, and finally to everyone's relief we feel the engine thrust reversing.

Hanoi at last, via twenty-four years of curiosity that amounts almost to yearning to just look at these men in their natural state. I have seen them before only as piled-up corpses at the edge of bomb craters or as frightened young men, hands tied behind them, being urged on by the muzzle of a South Vietnamese or American rifle. After spending so many years of being briefed on how they are the faceless menace or mindless pawns of evil masters or cowardly bastards who will not stand up and fight, I feel a need to engage them in the most banal kind of conversation. They of course turn out not to be the automatons that generations of State Department propagandists, aided by Hanoi's own inept efforts, would have had us believe. But when I go through the immigration and customs formalities at Noi Bai Airport, they seem to be doing their damnedest, as so often is the case, to live up to the portrait painted by their enemies. It is a thin effort. They are simply Vietnamese men, most of them too young to have been in the war, suppressing giggles as they peer at the ugly overcooked faces of these pudgy foreign devils. The devils in this case are a mixed bag of Australians, British, and Japanese diplomats, plus a group of international wise guys trying to sell the Vietnamese a fish-processing plant.

The police and customs uniforms have enormous Soviet-style shoulder boards that make the men look like little boys dressed up for a class play. But the attempt at Slavic severity dissolves into a Southeast Asian orgy of nose-picking, phlegm-collecting, and hacking up god knows what from the depths of their thin frames. I glide through immigration and customs formalities having been taken firmly by the elbow by Huang Mai Huong. She is to be my minder for this expedition. Miss Mai is twenty-seven, but looks seventeen. She is very tiny, very beautiful. She is dressed in the inevitable blue jeans and an expensive-looking top. Previous mindees, among them Dean Brelis, recently retired after a distinguished career at *Time* magazine, have been generous with gifts of clothing from Bangkok. Miss Mai could be a cheerleader at an Orange County high school. She is bouncy, full of spirit, with a smile that dazzles, but with eyes that can remain ice cold. She is the owner of a pass from the Foreign Ministry that can only be described as magic. One look and stern colonels melt. She spent seven years studying English at the Moscow Foreign Language Institute. She speaks it impeccably, or did until she began escorting Western camera crews, which have enriched her with phrases like: "I'm really pissed off."

I have had the foresight to bring along plenty of presents. All

4

Vietnamese love to give them and get them. I present Miss Mai with a box of Lindt Swiss chocolates, fresh from the Bangkok duty-free shop.

"Thank you sooo much," she says. "How did you know I was a chocolate freak? Wow!"

The ride into Hanoi is reminiscent of the ride into Manhattan from Kennedy Airport. The boulevard vies with the FDR Drive and the Ho Chi Minh Trail for cunningly arranged potholes. We rock around motorized cyclos and hordes of cyclists bent to their work.

Where on earth are these thousands of people going in the middle of the day? I discover that many of them will cycle thirty or forty miles simply to say hello to a cousin or to deliver some firewood to a sick granny. I decide that the Vietnamese have no sense of time the way we understand it, that their mental and body clocks are tuned more to history than to the ticking urgencies of ordinary life. That is why small, seemingly weak men and women were able to lug tons of supplies hundreds of miles through impassable and dangerous foot trails for years on end.

If time does not exist there is no cycle of work and reward. Or the reward is so small and remote or so large and abstract as to be the subject of polite conversation; as in "I hope the monsoon comes late this year," or "maybe the war will end in ten years or so."

My room at the Thong Nhat Hotel is as tired as I am. Gray, dead stucco walls, two massive bedsteads, each with a narrow straw mattress supported by a lattice of sagging strings. The bathroom is a complicated affair of exposed French plumbing fallen to rust and decay. I count five taps in the bath alone. The only one that works is the one marked *froid,* which from time to time emits lukewarm water. In the room there is no apparent source of heat. There is one broken air conditioner, which appears to have become that way because someone has put something—probably a foot—through its grillwork. There is a working refrigerator stocked with quarts of

5

beer, and from the ceiling hangs a single bare bulb on a twisted cord.

An interrogation room, I decide. Vietnam has been dogging me lately in the strangest way. It is flashback but not so highly charged and traumatic as the word suggests. This is different. This is something much more prosaic. There is some kind of formula at work here, some kind of periodic table. Vivid experience = zero. But vivid experience plus twenty years = brief pangs of guilt for so easily and effectively using, even exploiting, the deaths of so many and the danger to so many. Correspondents have been elevated to the status of hero for being mere bystanders. A once- or twice-a-week brush with the war and always a ticket home. We got awards and raises and hero-grams for telling an occasional truth and questioning a continuing lie. Lucky, arrogant bastards, most of us.

These feelings can be triggered by the most everyday sights. A young woman carrying a yoke of panniers filled with rice across a paddy with that fluid, spirited trot. She has the grace of a Makarova, but the effort I know is backbreaking. I suddenly find tears in my eyes.

All this has made for an extremely black mood, but Patti Hassler, the producer of this television visit, has a spirit about her that makes it dissolve. She is new to these parts and her curiosity and enthusiasm help me recognize it all for what it is. Just a damned good story.

8:00 P.M.: Dinner in Hanoi is awful. A mélange of various animals who've given up the ghost rather than forage the meager winter grasses of suburban Hanoi. It would be impossible to find such disgusting fare in Saigon. No Southerner would put up with such indifference. This dead stuff would be doctored, spiced, presented to give the illusion of something pleasurable. They just do not seem to care about things like pleasure in the North.

Late into dinner arrives Professor Nguyen Ngoc Hung, teacher of English at the Foreign Language Institute in Hanoi. He was a graduate student who was pressed into service in the manpower shortage that followed the North's dreadful losses in the Tet Offensive of 1968. Up to then he'd been given student exemptions. I am surprised to hear that there was such a thing in North Vietnam. Why is it we assume enemies cannot have lives at least as complicated as our own? In 1968 all student exemptions were canceled, which of course did not mean that everyone who was drafted necessarily went South. The children of party functionaries were drafted just like the rabble, but many of them managed to get assigned to strategy courses in Moscow or Beijing. There was not, as I understand it, any draft resistance in North Vietnam, but there was plenty of war avoidance.

Professor Hung is one of those delicate, almost effeminate men who on first meeting seem to be of the kind once seen in the pseudo French cafés of Saigon or Phnom Penh or behind the counters of boutiques on the Boulevard St. Michel in Paris. It is misleading. The fluttery hands and eyelids are the hesitations of a man who wants every one of his words to make perfect sense.

He is forty-one, has a wife and two sons, and has a hunger to speak English. Most of his days are spent with earnest undergraduates still at the *plume de ma tante* level of foreign language study. We agree to meet again.

January 19—5:30 A.M.: Hanoi is still in semidarkness when we leave the hotel for the long drive to the Thuan Thanh Institute. The bridges in and out of Hanoi are still guarded, one cannot imagine against whom. Is the ghost of General Curtis LeMay still roaming the skies of Hanoi? His suggestion to bomb the North back to the Stone Age, or more accurately, "to bomb until we have destroyed every work of man in North Vietnam," seems to have been superfluous. Time and neglect make a visitor feel the place is on the verge of collapse without any help from above. It all seems so ludicrous now, the idea that we were spending all that high explosive and those lives of pilots on what? On trying to make these Vietnamese into better people? Purging them of the dread disease of communism? If

7

punishment was necessary, the sheer drabness of the place is punishment enough. This is not the Vietnam I know. This is a furtive unapproachable city. The faces of the people resemble the façades of the shabby state shops. Shutters drawn, protecting empty shelves. I'm told that during the French colonial period it was a lovely sleepy town, built around a number of lakes. This morning it looks ugly and resentful, especially in this deserted dawn.

The drive takes us along pitted unpaved roads, through village markets offering bolts of blue cloth, handmade oil lamps, and not much more. A few pigs and a few muttering beetle-browed water buffalo.

As we pull into the institute, the director and staff are waiting to offer us tea and the inevitable briefing. Thuan Thanh Institute is a home for veterans who lost limbs or lost the use of their limbs. It includes men who lost the use of their minds as well. It is a drab and freezing place the government has stuck in a wilderness of rice paddies, an hour and a half from Hanoi.

There are perhaps twenty buildings made of crumbling cement blocks. Each building is divided into three rooms and each room contains three cots, three chipped enamel bedpans, and little else. The buildings are old and poorly constructed. Few of the windows have glass in them. Most have shutters that even when closed leave wide gaps between the rotting wooden slats. The rooms are damp and freezing cold. In the summer it must swarm with insects and stink to the heavens, surrounded as the place is by mounds of night soil. Some men seem permanently confined to their cots, but most are outside in a central campus. All are haggard, all have empty eyes, but all are grinning nonetheless and telling me how happy they are to be so well looked after.

Each is sitting on an ingenious tricycle. It is a tubular deck chair supported at the back by two large bicycle wheels and at the front by a smaller one. It can be propelled by two hand levers or by foot pedals. Everyone is very proud of these vehicles; both staff and patients boast they were designed by a veteran and built in Hanoi.

Morley Safer

Among the patients is Be Van Nhot. The poor fellow came within weeks of surviving intact. After spending five years in the South he stepped on a mine in what was almost the last battle of Vietnam, the siege of Ban Me Thuot. He suffered serious spinal injuries and lost the use of his legs just six weeks before Saigon fell. Mr. Nhot, which is how he refers to himself, wheels forward and explains that he speaks a little English. He is forty-two but looks sixty, so thin as to look emaciated. He has that concentration camp kind of boniness. His legs have almost completely wasted away.

I ask him about his unit, if he lost many friends in the war.

"At the beginning of the Ho Chi Minh campaign in 1975 we had twelve people in our squad. By the time I stepped on the mine we had lost five in Ban Me Thuot . . . when the mine went off three more were killed. So there is only me and another person left of that squad. Nobody won the war."

Mr. Nhot tells me he finds himself crying at night. "Some friend in the next room calls out: 'What . . . what happened, Mr. Nhot?' 'Oh, I have great fear!' "

Dr. Bui Tung, an orthopedic surgeon, is present during the walk through Thuan Thanh. For four years he was the director of a field hospital just a few miles north of the demilitarized zone, the DMZ, the boundary dividing North and South Vietnam. The doctor is a squat, academic-looking man who speaks in ornate and convoluted English.

"The wounded came in in a number of ways. The lucky ones came by truck up the Ho Chi Minh Trail. Others were brought up by riverboat. We also had two companies of special forces, about two hundred people. They would go down the trail with the soldiers, and after a battle they would carry the wounded back. They were well-meaning people, but we had terrible problems with them regarding our secrecy. They were noisy and talkative. Time and again we had to lecture them about the importance of security.

"We had one thousand beds in our hospital, but from the air you would not realize it. We had orders from our commander in chief,

9

General Giap, that no soldier must be wounded twice. So we put the most seriously wounded in underground bunkers. We put the others between the existing houses, then simply extended the roofs to cover them. The beds were scattered over six kilometers, among three different hamlets.

"The villagers helped to care for the wounded, and the lightly wounded would do odd jobs in the village, gather firewood, that sort of thing. Security was our biggest concern. I gave orders that there be no more cooking fires than there were before we moved in and that everyone—villagers and patients—must eat at the same time. I carried a weapon at all times, for there was great concern that the Americans would invade, either across the boundary or land from the sea."

Only one American "invaded" his hospital. A pilot, shot down less than a mile away, who parachuted into some tree and received minor injuries.

"The militia brought him in and bandaged him. I have never seen such fear as was in his face. He was so frightened; he tried to talk but no words came out. I think he feared that the militia would torture him when I was finished treating him."

I asked the doctor if he hated this man who only minutes before had been bent on killing him. "No, not anymore." The suggestion was that now he was just another harmless person who needed help.

"Do you remember his name?"

"No, I don't know his name, but I remember he was old for a pilot, well into his thirties, and he was from a place that sounded like a place in the Soviet Union."

"Georgia?"

"Yes, Georgia."

Last year, Dr. Bui Tung met more Americans. He was invited by the Joiner Center in Boston to attend a conference on the treatment of the severely wounded and the use of prosthetic devices. I am surprised to learn that many Vietnamese have visited the United

10

States. If there is an official invitation from a recognized organiza-tion, American authorities will grant a visa. If the guest is politically okay and the hosts pay all of his expenses, Hanoi will grant an exit visa. Bui Tung went from Boston to Washington, where, at Walter Reed Hospital, he met a number of American doctors who had served in Vietnam.

"They were anxious to know about all the places they remembered from the war. What was most interesting to me was that some of them had written papers for the *Journal of Bone and Joint Surgery*. During the war the *Journal of Bone and Joint Surgery* was very useful to me in treating the wounded. We were fighting each other with the same weapons and saving lives with the same medicine."

The good doctor is hungry for more medical journals. With the war over, the government's priorities have somehow shifted. They used to see to it that he received the latest American and British publications, but now orthopedics is not of the greatest importance. I promise I will send him some. Everyone in Vietnam is hungry for things to read.

We walk back to the car through this campus of the damned. The damp cold has that extra stab to it that is felt in such places as the north of England and Germany. The veterans smile at us through bad teeth. Those who can, wave . . . their shoulders hunched up against the chill. I am freezing with my gloves and woolen sweater and fully warranted hunting windbreaker. They sit in their aluminum chairs, twisted bodies protected only by old army tunics.

Their buddies carried these men back to the North for this. It is, I suppose, better than being left behind. I have been raised to believe that being locked away is a superior fate to being left to die. Looking at these men, I am not so sure.

Vietnam is a poor country. The North is an agony of poverty. But surely the place is not so poor that it must do this to these loyal men who have had their bodies broken so badly. Ho would be ashamed, I think.

11

The car is silent on the drive back to Hanoi. I feel as if I have wakened from a nightmare. I pinch my hands to assure them of their existence. The mind drifts, dozing. When I return from Vietnam I have another assignment, in Tucson. Another story involving an American veteran, a man from the Bronx who now lives out on the edge of the desert. He lost both arms, both legs, and an eye in Quang Nai Province. His name is Lloyd Kantor. As I drift off, bumping along the rutted road, I know that Lloyd Kantor and Mr. Nhot could engage in easy conversation. But what on earth would either man have to say to Dan Quayle? Genuine casualties are interesting people. Bad luck turns them into thinkers.

2

"Brother-Whose-Chin-Is-Up"

Hanoi, 11:00 A.M.: The message waiting at the hotel raises everyone's spirits. Giap will see us. I had been trying for weeks to get the Vietnamese Mission in New York to make this appointment, but they seemed reluctant to make the effort and were doubtful that anything would come of it.

Whatever juices remain of my years of daily news reporting are being stirred by the thought of sitting down with this legendary soldier, this architect of so much national pride and so much mourning.

The interview takes place in the old French governor-general's palace, an ornate colonial residence with a garden as overtended as any you would find in a Paris banker's weekend retreat.

Vo Nguyen Giap is almost eighty, looks very fit, and is beautifully tailored. He is very much the retired French general who looks and acts and even sounds like his old enemy, General Henri Navarre, the last commander of the French forces in Indochina. Giap whipped

13

him. At the time of the battle of Khe Sanh I flew to Nice to interview Navarre. It was that time when many people were making an easy and rather stupid comparison between the siege of U.S. forces at Khe Sanh and the French debacle of Dien Bien Phu. The only legitimate comparison that can be made is that in both battles the presidents of the United States, Dwight Eisenhower and Lyndon Johnson, considered using nuclear weapons to stop General Giap.

In his villa overlooking the Mediterranean, General Navarre told me that if only he had had more troops to throw into the slaughter, Dien Bien Phu would have been a victory and that he, Navarre, would have been proclaimed a hero. Giap, the victor, now appears to be as rejected after his glory years as the defeated Navarre was after his humiliation.

Giap has clearly been put out to pasture. He is nominally the deputy chairman of the Council of Ministers for Science and Technology, but has little, really, to do.

The trouble with generals is that they live in the big picture, and Giap, I decide, is a perfect example. Utterly brainwashed by ambition. Sending so many young men to die is never a matter of moral hesitation. It is, and especially in Giap's case, only a question of the strategy of the moment. It is as if all those lives were used to make a rather small point. Napoleon never hesitates. Brave men are the tools for carving one's initials in the pantheon.

Still, there is something tragically romantic about him. He was a farm boy whose father scrimped to send him to the best French schools in Hue and Hanoi. He is a living link in his nation's sorrowful victory. At high school in Hue he listened to lectures by Phan Boi Chau, the veteran nationalist who was allowed to leave house arrest to talk to students. By the time he graduated from law school he had become committed to Vietnam's independence. Any doubts about his commitment to rid his country of foreigners were swept away in 1941, when his wife and infant daughter died in a French prison and his sister-in-law was guillotined by the French in Saigon. Both

14

women had been active in the resistance to France. The child, of course, was yet another bystander. He is an inextricable part of the fabric of Vietnam, a fabric soaked in humiliation and triumph and the blood of millions.

I had mentioned to one of the crippled veterans at Thuan Thanh that I might be seeing Giap, and he said: "Please ask the heroic general if the General Offensive (the Tet Offensive) was worth it . . . tell him one of his soldiers, a lot of his soldiers, aren't sure."

When I tell Giap this story he dismisses it with a flourish I have seen only once before. Years ago, I interviewed Field Marshal Bernard Montgomery, the hero of El Alamein and no slouch in the business of committing other peoples' sons to battle. It is a movement of the back of the hand across the face . . . as one would discourage a pesky gnat.

It is only a matter of course, he tells me, "that each victory gained in war is worth the cost. Regardless of the cost.

"We paid a high price but so did you . . . not only in lives and matériel . . . do not forget the war was brought into the living rooms of the American people . . . the most important result of the Tet Offensive was it made you de-escalate the bombing, and it brought you to the negotiating table. It was, therefore, a victory."

I remind him that the popular wisdom is that in pure military terms Giap and his forces were utterly spent after Tet.

"The war was fought on many fronts. At that time the most important one was American public opinion. I will always respect the American people for their recognition that this was a war of aggression. Your soldiers fought very well, but they did not know why they were here. I have read the statements of your GIs. Your casualties were a waste of lives. Ours were martyrs to a cause. I don't think Westmoreland understood that."

"General Westmoreland writes that in a certain way he was envious of you, that you had the advantage of being able to conduct the war the way you saw fit."

15

"Ha! Your American generals don't read enough history."

I ask Giap about Westmoreland. What would have been the result had he been able to conduct the war his way, without the political considerations, without White House and congressional control over troop strength and even strategy.

"The result would have been worse," he says. "Your tragedy would have been greater. Read the Pentagon Papers . . . you will see Westmoreland wanted another two hundred thousand men. How many men would have been enough?"

The afternoon takes on a bizarre quality. Here is the author of so much American grief finding justification for his cunning in the enterprise of American reporters.

Giap continues: "But Westmoreland did not believe in human beings; he believed in numbers. He is a very responsible soldier, trained at the best military academies . . . but he did not understand the limitations of power in this war. He believed in weapons and matériel.

"Military power is not the decisive factor in war. Human beings! Human beings are the decisive factor." Giap's eyes crinkle and he smiles. A smile so big the eyes practically disappear.

Giap was regarded with awe by the American command. It considered him a genius of strategy in much the same way as the British general staff regarded Field Marshal Erwin Rommel, commander of the German Afrika Korps, the legendary Desert Fox. During the Second World War the British launched an unsuccessful commando raid to try to kidnap or, if necessary, to kill Rommel. In 1966 General Westmoreland put into operation a plan to kidnap General Giap.

American intelligence had reported to Westmoreland that the North Vietnamese had established a massive communications center on the Cambodian side of a point where the borders of Vietnam, Cambodia, and Laos converged. Giap, according to the reports, spent long periods at the center and had made it into his war room. The center was believed to be secured by at least one division of North Vietnamese troops.

16

Westmoreland asked American Special Forces to come up with a plan to invade the headquarters and extract Giap. A unit of 275 Montagnard tribesmen led by twenty-four American Green Berets was assembled and spent months training for the raid. Two nights before they were to set out the operation was canceled. Bad weather was blamed, but apparently wiser heads at Special Forces convinced Westmoreland that the operation was foolhardy, and although the troops might get into the center, they would never leave, with or without Giap. The unit, called the Mobile Guerrilla Force, was withdrawn and sent to the A Shau Valley.

I have never been able to determine the point of kidnapping Giap. It was as if by neutralizing him the enemy would fall into strategic disarray or their will to fight would be broken.

Armies often invest their enemies with almost superhuman powers. Giap did everything he could to encourage the myths that had grown up around him. To this day it is not even certain that a communications center existed or that Giap had ever used it.

I ask Giap how effective his intelligence on American operations was.

"I always had advance warning of the targets and the flight paths of the American bombers. We always knew when they were coming."

Perhaps he did, but it was almost unnecessary. When it was decided to expend more bombs on Vietnam than had been dropped anywhere in history . . . was it only six or was it seven million tons? . . . the targets become fairly predictable. Especially when the purpose is to destroy industrial targets in a nation whose main industry is rice production. The unwillingness of the Vietnamese to provide us with a wide choice of marshaling yards, petrochemical complexes, and armament factories produced a barely controlled frenzy among those who selected the targets, heaping more and more tonnage on the same unfortunate sites. A navy pilot wrote: "There were times when we would bomb the same railroad car fifteen times during the month. Each time the bomb assessment report was: 'target destroyed.'" In military jargon, it's called "making the rubble bounce."

17

As for civilians getting in the way, a number of pilots just dropped their loads in the South China Sea, and some others who didn't are still being eaten alive by the memory.

The doubtful were urged on by Scottsdale, Arizona's own Tamerlane, Barry Goldwater, who said: "You've got to forget about this civilian stuff."

I find that I have just foolishly written ". . . it was decided to expend more bombs . . ." Nothing of course was really decided. It just happened in the way best described by Royal Air Force pilots in the Second World War: ". . . out of the ashes of today's foul-up will rise the phoenix of tomorrow's fuck-up."

Americans making the rubble bounce and other such phoenixes made easy work for Giap's gunners. There was more than one "flak alley" in Vietnam, and we kept going back to them.

"That is why so many of your pilots did not come back; that is why so many were captured."

"What was the worst of it for you?"

"I confess it was the B-52 raids. Parts of the country looked like a moonscape. The men under my command in the South also had to face the B-52s, and for some it was very painful. But not for me. I was always optimistic. I was known as 'brother-whose-chin-is-up.'"

"I have studied the psychological research. Under bombing a human being may be sacrificed, but the spiritual strength to the nation of a human being can bring victory. Read Ho Chi Minh."

We go for a walk in the garden, and he agrees to talk to me in French.

"Ever a moment of conscience or pity, ever a regret about sending so many people to what you knew must be certain death?"

"Never. Not a single moment."

I had wanted to conduct the interview in French, but the man from the Foreign Ministry, a busybody of a fellow everyone knows as "Little Thach," insisted that it be conducted in Vietnamese and that he, Thach, be the translator. I later learn from Miss Mai, who

18

is a slave to accuracy-in-translation, that Thach mistranslated one of my questions. Giap's answer produced an amusing and telling response.

SAFER: "You're a very stubborn man, aren't you, General?" (The translator has me say: You're a very courageous man, aren't you, General?)

GIAP: "On that point . . . I once met Brzezinski, President Carter's National Security Adviser in Algiers, and he took me in both his hands and he said, 'I have long admired your courage, General Giap.'"

The story is plausible, Brzezinski would never lose an opportunity to ingratiate himself. I wonder what he would have said to Stalin?

Giap's demeanor is that of a wise schoolmaster lecturing a particularly dense student. He never achieved the status of Ho as father of independence, uncle to a nation. He is regarded as a soldier pure and simple, and a profligate one at that. But he tries hard to turn his boilerplate rhetoric about imperialism into gems of wisdom and advice.

"Americans are bad learners in the school of history . . . they should have known that I—the entire nation—would rather die than be enslaved. As Ho Chi Minh said, there is nothing sweeter than independence. A man who lives without freedom is not alive. Every chapter of our history is proof of that. You were invaders—we fought a war of national liberation."

"So, General," I ask, "do you think the Russians made the same mistakes in Afghanistan that the Americans made in Vietnam?"

The kindly uncle's face turns to granite.

"I think you should pose the question to our friends."

"A member of the Politburo once told me that the Soviet and

19

American interventions were doomed from the start for exactly the same reasons."

"It is a complicated question."

"But is the Afghan war not a war of national liberation?"

"We better return to Vietnam."

I present Giap with a copy of Neil Sheehan's book about John Paul Vann, *A Bright Shining Lie*. He is very pleased. He is also, he says, perplexed by the American obsession with Vietnam. But he tells me he has read every important book on the subject, from David Halberstam to Stanley Karnow.

Still cameras record the presentation. I must send Sheehan a photo. His meticulously written history of the false hero John Paul Vann being presented to this genuine article is an irresistible memento. One dazzling life built on folly and footwork and lies, the other on the bones of perhaps two million of "the sacrificed." Giap wants to talk some more. He has nothing else to do. But I leave him . . . quite a sad figure, really, this natty old man who loves to make war and loves even more to talk about it.

Duff Cooper, the British soldier-diplomat, borrowed from Shakespeare's *Henry V* for the title of his memoir *Old Men Forget*.

Unfortunately, they do not.

3

"You, Sir, Are Collapsed"

2:00 P.M.: The drive from the Thong Nhat Hotel to the Park of the B-52s takes us through the deserted side streets of Hanoi. The rain is coming down in brief, furious squalls, giving the city the look of a wet Sunday. Hanoi, at least these parts of it, seems more like a run-down industrial suburb of Brussels or London than the capital of an Asian nation. There is none of the rich, gabby, food-oriented street life of Hong Kong or Bangkok or Saigon.

The park is a vast grassland of Soviet-made antiaircraft weapons and broken American airplanes.

It is an eerie place. High-tech tombs for young men who loved speed, danger, and the idea of duty. The place is haunted by, among other things, language. The various bits of sheet metal still carry indecipherable military nomenclature, plus more translatable words like NO STEP and DANGER. Children play war games on these wrecks or use them as interesting obstacles for climbing. Our swords have been beaten into jungle gyms.

21

I am here to meet Bui Tin, age sixty-two. Colonel, People's Army of Vietnam (Ret.). He has the face of a Maquisard, which of course is exactly what he was for thirty-seven years of his life. When I say this to him, he corrects me. "Actually thirty-seven years and four months," he says.

He is wearing a trench coat and a navy blue beret, and like so many Vietnamese he chain-smokes. He reminds me of a scaled-down version of the late Edward G. Robinson, the actor. He started his career fighting the French.

He was wounded seven times, three times in the French war, including a head wound at the battle of Dien Bien Phu, and four times in the American war. He was hit twice at Khe Sanh, again at Dak To in the highlands, and once again in the last few days of the war. He confesses he was never very political, but in 1945, like most of his classmates at the French *lycée* in Hue, he got caught up in a tide of nationalism. Perhaps he was not political, but dependable enough to be named deputy editor of *Nhan Dan,* the Army newspaper, when he retired.

"When I was seventeen I wanted to go to France to study philosophy. I thought I would do that as soon as the war with France was over," he says.

"But somehow it never happened." He says he is like the country: ". . . tired . . . tired of war." Maybe so, but I get the impression that he was very good at soldiering the way some people are good athletes. He is quick and strong and very stubborn.

I ask him about that quality in the Vietnamese character. Is that what made them so effective in so many wars? "You must understand," he says, "most of our soldiers are farm people. The degree of education is not high, and the condition of life is very, very hard. All they have is the spirit of independence. That has been constantly challenged. Someone has always wanted to take that last thing away from them. The Chinese, the French, the Americans. Even the Americans came all that distance to take this last thing away from them."

22

"We heard all kinds of stories during the war about the conditions on the Ho Chi Minh Trail. How difficult was it for you as a commander to keep men motivated?"

"It was not hard because our men had an idea, a cause. We used the Henry Kissinger philosophy. He said that if the Americans weren't winning, they were losing . . . we lived by the principle that if we weren't losing, we were winning. As for the conditions on the Ho Chi Minh Trail, I cannot describe to you the inner strength that our soldiers showed. They would march for twelve hours and then spend another two hours digging in.

"A man could lose two hundred grams of blood every day from the leeches. The leeches have an anticoagulant . . . many of my men bled to death. Food was a constant worry, especially for the big units. I remember we shot an elephant once, and for five days we had meat. Men drowned; they fell off cliffs; they died of malaria and snake bites. I used to look up in the sky and envy you in those helicopters."

The Americans, he tells me, fought well in large battles but were not so effective in small-unit operations. The thing that puzzles him most is the one-year tour of duty.

"Our soldiers had no fixed term for their duty. They knew they had to fight until the war was over. You send a man here for one year. Only one year! He spends six months learning; for three months he is a good fighter, but for the last three months he is trying to protect himself to make sure he stays alive. About the time he was ready to fight, he was ready to leave! I do not understand such a policy."

The one-year tour of duty was General Westmoreland's idea, or so he claimed during the war. Charles Collingwood and I spent an evening with him just before Christmas of 1966, and over dinner the general mused on about how high the morale of American troops was in Vietnam. Collingwood asked if one year was an efficient use of manpower.

"Oh yes," said Westmoreland. "These young men are working hard and fighting hard and putting their hearts and souls into it for a year. I could not be more proud of their commitment to this war."

23

He also said that by spreading out the duty there would be less pressure in the United States to "bring the boys home."

He did not seem to realize that by spreading the duty he was exposing more and more Americans to the disenchantment and sense of uselessness that were infecting his troops. Drugs were already becoming a problem in the field, and there is no way Westmoreland could not have been aware of it. "Fragging" too had begun . . . the rather unsporting practice among draftees of rolling a fragmentation grenade into the tent of a sleeping officer.

For a career soldier Westmoreland had a curiously corporate view of the war. He seemed to regard it as a production and distribution exercise, placing full faith in the computer printout of the moment and the tonnage of artillery shells spent. Although no doubt he was courageous in battle in the Second World War and in Korea, as a commander in Vietnam he was a simpering toady when dealing with the White House and the Defense Department. If, as he later claimed, he was hamstrung by amateurs in Washington, he was equally hamstrung by his own ambition. He confided to Charles and me that night in his headquarters in Saigon that he would not say no if offered the chance to be a candidate in the presidential election of 1968. Perhaps it was the expectation of such an opportunity that prevented him from doing the decent soldierly thing and quitting. Americans fought well in Vietnam. Remarkably well, for an army that was at the top either blind or morally bankrupt.

However merciless Giap seemed with his lack of doubt about sending so many young people to their deaths, it was matched by Westmoreland's plain ignorance and insensitivity. In 1966 I had been accompanying him around the country on a tour of American bases, and over lunch I mentioned to him that the previous day I had been to the funeral of a young Vietnamese soldier. The family was in a frenzy of grief, and at the cemetery I was absolutely shattered by the sight of what seemed to be a thousand coffins being prepared for burial. I asked Westmoreland about the dreadful losses the South Vietnamese army was suffering.

24

"Oh yes," he said. "But you must understand that they are Asians, and they don't really think about death the way we do. They accept it very fatalistically."

This was a widely held attitude among many Americans in Vietnam, including a number of journalists. It was partly racism—"they're only gooks"—and partly that ancient defense mechanism of war, which is to reduce the enemy to a subspecies. In the case of Vietnam it was necessary also to include the "puppets," given that many were the sons and cousins of the people we were trying to kill.

As common as the attitude was, I was surprised to hear it articulated by a four-star general. The sheer thickheadedness of this well-meaning man was appalling.

Bui Tin, like every Vietnamese veteran I talked to, recalls the terror of the B-52 raids. "In the French war I caught a bomb fragment in the head and couldn't sleep for three months. I had no wounds from the B-52 raids, but the psychological problems for me and my men were terrible. You cannot understand what it was like unless you've lived through it.

"The bombs came out of absolute silence. And because you had no warning and could see nothing because of the dust, you did not know which way to run until the second stick of bombs exploded. The only tactic we could use was to spread out in as many directions as possible. You could always tell who among the troops had been through a B-52 attack—they would take off after every loud noise."

"The men who served under your command, the ones who survived, have they managed to cope with peace?"

"There are a lot of psychological problems; the same ones as your veterans. Nightmares, a number of suicides. But the biggest problems were family problems. Many of our men fought in the South for ten, even fourteen years. Can you imagine what that does to a marriage? The older veterans are the ones who suffered the most."

"How about you?"

He laughs. "I still have the B-52 problem; I sometimes panic when I hear a loud noise."

25

"Was that the worst part of the war for you?"

"No, the worst was the American counteroffensive after Tet, 1968. We took terrible losses, and if there was any doubt at all, it was in those months after Tet. We had to completely reorganize in the South. We had to send sixteen- and seventeen-year-olds down. That part was terrible."

"Was the Tet Offensive a mistake?"

"No, the losses were great, but the effect was to demoralize the American people . . . the Americans had to reorganize too . . . they withdrew from Vietnam."

Bui Tin smiles a lot. The impression is that, as fierce a fighter as he is, he looks back with nothing more than pride in a job well done. Still some nightmares about the price that was paid, but on balance it was all worth it. I doubt whether many divisional commanders, on either side, had this man's quality and thoughtfulness.

It was Bui Tin who took the surrender of Saigon from that last laugh of the Republic of South Vietnam, General Duong Van Minh—known to everyone as "Big Minh." He had been involved in the assassination of Ngo Dinh Diem and had once been chief of state. He continued to plot against a variety of South Vietnamese administrations, usually with the support of the United States. He was a man who spent most of his life waiting in the wings for a call to power. The call finally came in April 1975, when he became the third president of the country in the last ten days of its life. It was the last great hope of the French and Americans that Big Minh represented a "third force." A man who could negotiate with Hanoi to keep some kind of southern entity alive. I ask Bui Tin about that day:

"Big Minh approached me. He was the last president. He says, 'Good morning. I have been waiting for you, sir, to transfer power.' I told him . . . you have nothing to transfer . . . you have no power in your hand. You, sir, are collapsed."

When I ask him who won the war, he laughs out loud. "No one really won," he says; ". . . the United States lost."

26

Morley Safer

I recall the faces of those crippled veterans in their pitiful hostel near Hanoi. I asked Bui Tin what he would say to those men who fought so hard for so long and gave so much . . . for so little reward.

"I would quote to them the American Declaration of Independence . . . just as Ho Chi Minh did. There is nothing more precious than independence."

"Does that make you a good Nationalist or a good Communist?"

Bui Tin responds with a great snorting horselaugh and a look that says: What a question, so typically American. And he answers slightly wearily: "A Nationalist. I've always been a Nationalist . . . the communism came later . . . I think it is what you call an afterthought."

The sun seems never to shine in Hanoi in January . . . standing under glum skies in that park that had dead aircraft instead of trees, mobile SAM missiles and antiaircraft cannon instead of jungle gyms, I feel very old talking to this old soldier and as irrelevant as the remains of the B-52s. Two relics of the Children's Crusade, one a witness, the other a leader . . . both tired yet excited by all this war talk.

I ask him if he has heard or read about the Vietnam Memorial in Washington.

"Yes, yes, I have been to it . . . also the memorial in New York."

I am jolted by this piece of information. I wonder what those veterans who still visit the wall in their old Vietnam fatigues would have done, or thought, had they known that the squat man in the beret was possibly responsible for the presence of some of those fifty-eight thousand names on the wall.

"It is very important, the wall. All the memorials. You must remember all those young men . . . you must look at those names and wonder how many doctors and scientists, maybe even a philosopher. You must also remember the kind of bravery those young men had. They may not have had much understanding of the aims of that war. But the sacrifice, so much sacrifice, must not be forgotten. The spirit of young people must not be forgotten.

27

"I cannot forget ours. A young man who is asked by his country to go and kill must be very brave. It is not a natural thing to ask of a person."

I walk to the car with Bui Tin, and the day takes an even more manic surrealistic turn when he tells me: "It was so exciting visiting the United States. I got to see my sister in Los Angeles."

Morley Safer

4

"The Guitar Went Too"

7:00 P.M.: I am sitting in my room at the Thong Nhat, committing the sin that offers no pardon. Drinking alone. As cheerless as this room is, it is preferable to the grubbiness of the bar downstairs. I am waiting for Professor Nguyen Ngoc Hung, the delicate young man who did his duty. He put down his books; put on rubber tire sandals—"Ho sandals"; picked up his Kalashnikov, the standard issue AK-47 assault rifle and three clips for it, a bayonet, three grenades, a water bottle; and strapped on a fifty-five-pound pack that included a poncho and hammock but mainly contained rice to eat along the way and started walking South with orders to kill as many Americans and their puppets as possible.

It was not quite so simple as that, but almost. The hard part for me to understand is the idea of duty to a country that is waging a war of stubbornness . . . a war being fought, once you get past the slogans, to prove you can whip technology with sandals, and incidentally a million or so lives. Sitting in this damp room, "liberation"

29

seems the least of it. The profoundly unliberated walk as much as a thousand miles to liberate the equally unliberated, to kill them when necessary, and to kill perfect strangers who've flown thirteen thousand miles to do the same.

Liberation, I think, is the Shroud of Turin of our age. Even the true believers know it is bunk, but it's the kind of bunk that pulls people out of farms and classrooms.

Wretched Professor Hung. I get the feeling that he is not fully trusted in Hanoi; his English is too good. He tells me he is not happy when he visits Ho Chi Minh City: "I feel strange there, you know . . . people are very forward and they speak roughly." I suspect he also feels there are too many diversions in the South, distractions from his Melville and Dickens. He lost a brother in the war; he knows not where. This eats him up . . . Vietnam is too big a land, too vast a cemetery to find him . . . to do the right thing, to tend a grave, to commemorate a death-day.

We are sitting in a corner of my room sipping scotch and chasing it with Heineken. I ask Hung if the people in Hanoi, the other students, have any idea how bad the casualties were in the Tet Offensive.

"Very few people talked about the casualties at Tet . . . but I had an uncle who was in it, and he came back with a leg missing. He told me how bad it was. Still, we were anxious to go. We were ready to pick up our studies later. They had some old soldiers who had already been South prepare us for the trip down. They were tough. They made us ride bicycles over rough ground with very heavy loads. They explained to us what life would be like in the jungle. I was born in the city . . . it took me some time to adapt. I was not really very strong. The whole operation, the march down South, was for me personally a physical triumph."

I think of the American recruits arriving in Vietnam and the paraphernalia they brought with them, the small comforts, guitars and boom boxes and portable television sets. And the large comforts the

30

Pentagon provided. Long Binh army post, sixteen miles from Saigon, was a city of twenty-six thousand American support troops. In 1970, when four hundred thousand American soldiers were in the country, only seventy-five thousand were considered combat troops. Life in Long Binh compelled me to broadcast a report called "Oh, What a Lovely War for Some." In it the post's operations officer, a Captain Edward Moore, catalogued the camp's amenities.

"Well, here at Long Binh we have about the same facilities you might find stateside. We have eight Olympic-sized swimming pools. We have ranges for archery and skeet shooting. For golf we have putting and driving ranges. And we are building a couple of bowling alleys. And of course there is basketball. We have only four football fields, and right now we don't have enough people to referee the games.

"There's a lot of roads to run around for people who want to keep in shape. They have to use their initiative, you know, and go to special services and find things to do. There's plenty to do; there's no real cause for complaint."

The captain did not include in his list the "American-style" Chinese restaurant or the two brothels operated by outside contractors.

Twenty-two thousand Vietnamese workers were brought on the base each day to service the needs of the twenty-six thousand Americans. Support troops for the support troops.

After six months in Vietnam, all servicemen were given a week's vacation outside the country. It was called R and R—Rest and Recuperation. The GIs called it Rape and Run.

I ask Hung what comforts he had along the trail.

"Before we left, I brought my dictionaries, novels, diaries, and my guitar . . . but carrying all that load . . . the first to go were the dictionaries, then the novels, then the diaries . . . and last of all, the guitar went too."

"Did you have any kind of support system?"

"There were places we would stop and rest for a day, and some of

31

them had repair shops for the antiaircraft weapons, and others had rice and salt for us."

"What about mail . . . messages from home?"

"For us? No, never for us. Some of us brought along with us letters we received from sweethearts before we left for the South. We passed them among ourselves and read them aloud and laughed and teased each other with some of the things girlfriends say to soldiers going off to war."

He pauses, a half smile on his face, as he recalls with pleasure those fleeting distractions from the endless trek. "It was nice, sharing feelings, sharing sentiments. Those letters were very precious, we never knew when we would get another letter . . . *if* we would get another letter."

"Was the fighting what you expected? Were you prepared for it?"

"For the fighting, yes . . . but not for the B-52s . . . there is nothing that can prepare you for that. The first time they came I remember the place went absolutely silent. Normally there was some kind of aircraft around if we were anywhere near a battle. It was a wonderful day, not a sound, nothing but birds and insects, and I remember watching bombs fall, and they seemed to fall slowly, and they grew bigger and bigger. And we were fascinated because they took on different shapes as they fell. And then there was nothing; we could hear nothing or see nothing. The dust and the smoke were everywhere . . . it was night in the middle of the day. Two of my closest friends died."

Professor Hung's eyes go moist, and for a moment he cannot talk.

"I actually had to bury them. There is no other way, you know. Mark the grave with something and then keep moving. If the helicopters were around, you could not even do that. The worst was the B-52. After the B-52 raids you go around and gather up the bits, the pieces of the bodies, and you try to bury them."

I remember going for one of those "walks in the sun," I think with the 25th Infantry Division. Two things happened that day. A mortar

32

round fell short and killed someone up ahead and wounded two or three others . . . and farther along we came through the "carpet" that a B-52 strike had laid. The stench was beyond all belief. The bombers had gotten very lucky. One bomb had cratered a command bunker. The maggots had already taken over. Farther along there was a pile of bodies near a cooking fire. They were perfectly intact North Vietnamese regulars. Fully uniformed, some of them had their pith helmets still in place. They must have been killed by blast or pressure. I recall thinking they looked much larger, stouter than most Vietnamese. The internal gases, of course, were beginning to swell the bodies.

The American war—at least the system that supported it, the so-called logistics—was an orderly affair. The arrival of beans and bullets, the departure of bodies, all happened on time.

The dead especially were treated with urgent tenderness. Careful hands zipped them into body bags. Helicopters brought them to airfields, where they were picked up by C-130 transports that flew them to Tan Son Nhut, where they were received by civilian morticians who had successfully bid for the contract.

The man who ran the mortuary at Tan Son Nhut, a beet-faced cracker, insisted one day that I come in. He wanted to show me something "interesting." Under a transparent plastic shroud was the bloated body of a young man.

"Sumpthin', eh?" he said.

"Yeah," I said, feeling slightly ill from the unmistakable aroma that hung in the room.

"Know who it is?"

"No."

"Tab Hunter's brother. Imagine, Tab Hunter's brother, right here in my place. Drownded."

The morticians did what morticians do and carefully sealed the bodies in heavy aluminum coffins, double-sealed, as demanded by the international agreement for the transportation of corpses.

33

They were then flown home and buried with a military honor guard in attendance. There was no such luxurious departure for the other side. Professor Hung lost a brother. He does not know where or when.

"We were called up in the same month, but he went South before me. A year after he left he died, but that is all the information we have. My father would like to find him, but I have to explain to him how difficult it is to find someone buried in the tropical forest. My father cried for days. This is not usual for a man in Vietnam. But you know, we worship the dead. It is very important for my father and for me to know—even the day he died, but we do not. We will never know."

Professor Hung, eminent teacher of English, recipient of a British Council scholarship to study at London University, winner of a teaching grant to spend a year in Australia, becomes, in this awful room in Hanoi, Poor Soldier Hung; the awkward city boy who tried to bring his dictionaries and guitar to war. He sips his scotch and cries a little.

5

Homecoming

Hanoi, January 20, 6:00 A.M.:   I am pleased to be leaving Hanoi. Even after a few days the city has become a dank oppressive cloak.

It is probably only in my mind, but as the Russian-made Air Vietnam turboprop descends on Saigon, everyone's spirits seem to lift. I know it is no more meaningful or symbolic than geography ever is, but fittingly, the city is bathed in sunshine. It is not, of course, Saigon anymore. It is Ho Chi Minh City. Tan Son Nhut Airport is as it was twenty years ago, only less so. The helicopter and fighter-bomber revetments are empty. Behind a low wall there is a line of Russian military helicopters quickly becoming victims of the damp and mold.

The airport lounge buzzes with high spirits. Nothing dour about these Southerners. There is a sprinkling of airport taxi hustlers who would not last a minute in Hanoi but who would be perfectly at home at Kennedy Airport. I scan the crowd looking for a familiar face.

35

I have been to this place hundreds of times . . . but the last time was seventeen years ago. Always, there were people I knew, people who could help. Drivers, airline clerks, baggage handlers. I am disappointed. Not even a blink of recognition. Why is it we expect time to freeze in our absence? Is it some juvenile instinct?

The official purpose of this visit is to report for *60 Minutes.* I have my own agenda. I want to discover my reaction to this "homecoming." I expect to be deeply saddened by this place that suffered so much by its own hand and by the hands of perfect strangers. I expect to be regarded with suspicion and to be set upon emotionally.

In fact, Ho Chi Minh City barely notices me. The place is as lively and rambunctious as it was during the worst wise-guy days of the war. It also looks better than I remember it. The trip in from Tan Son Nhut is quick and tidy. No fuming military convoys, just an orderly stream of bicycle traffic and cyclos.

Ho Chi Minh City is, I suspect, becoming Saigon once again. The Saigon between-the-wars. A city trying to get its identity back or at the very least to find a new one. It will certainly never be the wicked and joyful place it was or the honky-tonk we turned it into, and above all I cannot imagine it becoming like Hanoi. Never.

The check-in process at the old Majestic Hotel, now the Cuu Long, is as smooth as if it were the Ritz in Paris. The assumption by the clerks is that you will pay your bill when you check out, so like the Ritz, or the Ritz I remember, all that is needed is a simple signature. No fumbling with credit cards, no officious, "May I imprint you, sir?" from some freeze-dried Hilton-trained Muppet.

I excuse myself from the minders and the CBS caravan.

I walk through blocks familiar to a generation of reporters and soldiers. The tarts have gone from Tu Do Street, their haunts replaced by lacquer shops that seem to exist only to hawk black-market dong, the currency that has replaced the old Vietnamese piaster. The old café Givral, where at breakfast they served the best *soupe Chinois* in Saigon, now has little more on the menu than eggs. Utterly indifferent young women run the place.

Brodard, the other slightly raffish Left Bank café on Tu Do Street, has kept its standards up under what surely are extremely trying conditions. The same old manager is there, although now he seems to be a waiter. He offers a choice of things but strongly indicates that the best he can do is a grilled chicken. There is a lot of spirited banter between him and the women behind the bar, and the food, though limited, is still excellent. The staff makes a genuine effort to please. A few other tables are occupied by a slightly less flamboyant version of what we used to call Saigon Cowboys, slick young men who avoided the draft, drove souped-up cars, and wore clothes from Paris. They are still around, or their younger brothers are. They drive mopeds and wear clothes from Bangkok. Someone suggests they are children of important party people, but I have no proof of this.

6

The Logic of Dr. Hoa

3:00 P.M.: Even the smartest of us knew so little. I am reflecting on this nugget of cheap wisdom sprawled on a park bench within the lush inner courtyard of the old Grall hospital in Ho Chi Minh City. I have been here before. I once watched in fascination as a team of American doctors, protected by sandbags, removed a live grenade from under the rib cage of an old Vietnamese farmer. The unfortunate man had left his hut in the middle of the night for a pee, and a nervous sentry shot him with an M-79 grenade launcher. The grenade pierced him but did not explode, and the poor fellow, this living bomb, had walked all the way to Saigon, perhaps fifteen miles, to complain about this pain in his side.

When the doctors removed the missile and sewed him up, he hopped off his cot and walked back home.

My thought for the day has gurgled up in anticipation of an appointment I have at the hospital with Dr. Duong Quynh Hoa, who conducts a daily maternity clinic here. She is one of the sixteen

Morley Safer

founders of the National Liberation Front, the Vietcong. The party was organized at a secret meeting in Cu Chi in 1960.

Even the smartest of us knew so little. The State Department and the White House had reduced the mission to Vietnam to a crusade, the easiest kind of equation for soldiers and reporters to understand. The orders are simple: kill or convert heathen or Communists. It makes knowing the enemy secondary to killing him, or in today's case, her . . . and it makes for dangerous delusions. The crusade denied contradiction in a society that had made contradiction its one unshakable precept.

Dr. Hoa was born into a rich and prominent Saigon family. Her father was one of the few "natives," as the French referred to all Vietnamese, to hold a teaching post at the *lycée* in Saigon. In spite of the family's assimilation into French society, it maintained a strong nationalist spirit. Dr. Hoa was sent to high school in France and then on to medical school in Paris, where she joined the French communist party. In 1954 she returned to Vietnam, where she practiced pediatrics and worked covertly recruiting intellectuals for the revolution. She is a plump, jolly woman in her middle fifties who speaks passable English; she prefers to speak to me in French.

"My politics were never really a secret," she says. "I was open in my opposition to Diem and the Americans who supported the régime. I suppose because I was a doctor and everyone knew me that they assumed I was nothing more than a rich café radical. After all, I came from an assimilated bourgeois family, what we used to call 'collaborationist,' so it was expected that the foreign-educated daughter would be a little bit red, a little bit of a rejectionist, but not much more than that. Actually, it was an excellent cover for my activities. Had I been anticommunist, it would have been surprising."

In 1960 she was arrested and questioned about her political activities by the Saigon police. She was not tortured, she says, because of the influence of her family and because she was the pediatrician for the children of most of the politicians.

39

Dr. Hoa worked in Saigon through the middle 1960s, became very friendly with the American embassy, with both Ambassadors Lodge and Taylor, and met General Westmoreland a number of times on the Saigon cocktail circuit.

"So you were a spy?"

"Of course I must be frank and say yes. But they were still my friends. The English and French ambassadors too."

In 1968, after Tet, Hanoi ordered her to take to the jungle, to the Vietcong base in Tay Ninh. She lived in the jungle with her husband, a mathematician, treating the wounded and making policy. After Saigon fell she was named a Heroine of the Revolution and made deputy minister of health; she was one of the few Southerners to be given a position of importance.

In 1979 she left the party, thoroughly disillusioned with what she called the second-rate people who had taken over. She looks more than a little wistful when she tells me that "something goes wrong at a certain age. You stop seeing things as clearly at forty as you did at twenty-one. I thought I was making a revolution for the people . . . I know that sounds very idealistic, but you must understand how determined we were. I discovered that I made a revolution for a cause, for a discipline, for an ideology. The people had nothing to do with it. I have no regrets because it was necessary above all to get the foreigners out of our country."

This sophisticated, compassionate woman can be very tough. When I ask her what the worst moment of the war was, she tells me of two.

"My brother was a lawyer in Dalat. In 1965 the Thieu soldiers came and murdered him with a machine gun, in front of his house, in front of his family. He was a lawyer, but he worked for the revolution."

"That was 1965, the time of the American buildup. Did you hate the Americans then?"

"No, because it was logical, the murder of my brother."

"Logical?"

40

"In the context of war, it is perfectly logical."

I knew this story of her brother from the research notes that Patti Hassler had given me. I was not surprised, given the political background of her family. But quite suddenly, in the middle of a rather rambling interview, Dr. Hoa's eyes fill with tears.

"The saddest experience was the death of my son, my only child. He died in the jungle where it was not possible to treat him. He died of encephalitis. But it was a little experience when I compare it with any of our fighters."

I try to offer something, some phrase that might ease the pain that was now so evident from the tears running down her cheeks. Or perhaps I said it to ease the shock I felt.

"Not so little an experience . . . one death can be harder to understand than . . ."

She interrupts me . . . wipes her eyes, and her face hardens as quickly as it had given in to tears.

"It is only one death. One death in about a million deaths."

"Was it worth it? Was it worth that one death?"

"Yes."

I can only imagine what is going on in this woman's mind. The country's most eminent pediatrician, unable to save the life of her own child, lying in a jungle hammock. A child dying for a cause she has come to no longer really believe in.

What seems to be at work is a fierce and unforgiving process that she would call "logic." It leaves only moments for sentiment, happiness, or even grief.

Her job just after the Tet Offensive was to help smuggle Vietcong out of Saigon back to bases near Cu Chi and farther west, to Tay Ninh. She will not tell me what part she played in infiltrating VC units into the city before the offensive began. But it clearly became too hot for her to remain after Tet, so she stayed in Tay Ninh with other members of the Politburo. She talks about the seven years in the jungle with something approaching nostalgia.

"It was so easy to motivate people. Imagine what it must be like

41

to be fighting the most powerful people in the world and to know in your heart that you are winning and that the cause is just. It enabled us to laugh at the B-52 raids, at least after the raids, when you felt so lucky to be alive.

"It is not so easy to motivate the people in peace. I used to tell it to my friends in the Politburo when I still belonged to the party. I guess we lost the peace.

"Many of my friends feel deceived. I don't; I guess I expected it."

She is talking about how the party changed and how the Northerners tried to impose rules on the stubborn and diverse Southerners.

"The men from Hanoi lived under communism for thirty-five years, but the people in the South have had different kinds of lives."

She fudges her answer when I ask her if the North has abused its power.

"I think power is a very dangerous thing."

Dr. Hoa tells me that the Northerners are regarded as another invader, another usurper.

"They have no idea how to function in peace. The people they sent down here were military. They do not know how to run a factory or a hospital. All they know is war and political indoctrination."

In Ho Chi Minh City there are stories of official corruption, of party officials selling exit visas, of the children of Politburo members importing expensive European and Japanese cars.

Dr. Hoa says she keeps in touch with a lot of the "fighters." "They are having a very difficult time. They still cannot talk to their families about the war. In some cases close relatives were in the Saigon army and sent away for ten or twelve years of reeducation, and they were not able to help them. This has given them yet another burden to carry.

"The veterans feel forsaken, abandoned. They are poor, they cannot find jobs, they have the most serious psychological problems. They abuse their wives and their children. Many lost their wives during the war. One friend of mine is now an ambassador, but while

42

he was fighting in the jungle, his wife ran off with an American. Nobody won this war, nobody."

Throughout our interview, a slim middle-aged man has been standing off to one side trying hard to give the appearance that he is not listening to every word. I assume he is a party or city official or some hospital functionary charged with reporting everything the doctor has said. As we leave I approach and introduce myself, but he backs off, almost furtively.

"Are you with the hospital?" I ask.

"Yes, I am in charge of foreign liaison for Dr. Hoa's clinic."

"You work for the government?"

"No, I work for Dr. Hoa personally. She is the only one who would give me a job in 'liberated' Vietnam."

The man's English is almost flawless. I ask him where he learned it.

"I taught English for many years in Saigon in a private school that was owned by Captain Linh."

Captain Linh was a wealthy, charming air force officer, a sidekick and public relations man to Air Marshal Nguyen Cao Ky, chief of the air force and later prime minister. They were quite dashing—Ky in his purple jumpsuit and pearl-handled revolver, Linh always in perfectly tailored uniforms or Italian suits. Linh's schools prospered in the sixties, when it became clear to many Vietnamese families that English was the language of success. Captain Linh, like Marshal Ky, was evacuated before the fall of Saigon. This English teacher was not so lucky.

"I was called up by the army in 1968; I tried to get a deferment, but I did not have enough influence. I was sent to New Jersey in 1970 to an advanced radio operations school. That was the biggest mistake of my life, to go to the United States.

"When Saigon fell I was arrested like most of the other officers, but because of my year in America, they sent me to reeducation camp for four years. It was slave labor, purely and simply, with only enough rations to stay alive, barely alive.

43

"When I got out I couldn't get work of any kind. I tried to explain to them that they were wasting the talent of a perfectly good teacher, that I was not political in any way. I had never been political; all I ever wanted to do was teach. I was never a member of any party. To my shame I can say I was never even a Nationalist. But it was no use. Our new masters don't think education is very important.

"I tried for every kind of job, even the most menial, but somehow just by looking at me they knew I had been in the camp. No one would take the risk, except for Dr. Hoa; she is the only one who would defy them. The pay is not good, but at least I am working, and I have some pride. She is a remarkable woman."

7

"Top of the World"

6:00 P.M.: The bar of the Majestic—the Cuu Long—is a cheery place that in the evening carries a faint memory of the ground floor of the old Continental Palace, now closed for renovation. It has none of the palm-fronded colonial decadence of the Continental, but there is the same sense, at this hour of the day, of people gathering to gossip about the frailties of this or that ministry. A nice breeze is coming off the river, and the "golden hour" of the tropics is beginning to darken.

I am sipping tea with Professor Hung, who, despite his earlier reservations about Ho Chi Minh City, seems to be thoroughly enjoying himself. I suspect this has as much to do with the opportunity to speak in English without lecturing in it, as with any of the temptations of this easygoing city.

There is a clublike atmosphere to the place, and various Americans and even a few Vietnamese-Americans who are here visiting relatives drop by the table just to make amiable conversation. The professor seems to have overcome his dour Victorian upbringing in gloomy Hanoi.

We brought Professor Hung with us to Ho Chi Minh City in order to get him back to Quang Tri City, just south of the old DMZ. He had fought in the battle of Quang Tri, and we want to walk over the ground together as well as visit the cemetery at Trung Son, where ten thousand or more of his comrades are buried. With Air Vietnam's zany schedule, it is necessary to fly fifteen hundred miles to get to a destination only five hundred miles from Hanoi.

A group of American veterans, from an outfit called "Vets with a Mission," are in Ho Chi Minh City. They have been touring the country, more as an attempt to heal themselves than out of any curiosity about Vietnam. There is a whiff of born-again-ism about them, but they are not wild-eyed or out to save the world or even their old enemies. They are mainly trying to save themselves. Their collective wounds are horrifying. There are eight in all plus one former construction worker from RMK, Raymond Morrison & Knudson, the contractor that got very rich building the airstrips, base camps, and just about everything that would not move in Vietnam. I don't know what he is doing here. Is he feeling guilty about the quality of the cement work? He should. In fact, there is nothing funny about civilians or anyone having serious post-Vietnam blues. I know of a former air force sergeant who spent the war at Dover Air Force Base in Delaware and is having bad postwar problems: nightmares, flashbacks, the lot. He spent his year unloading coffins.

The leader of the group is Bill Kimball, who in 1968 was an eighteen-year-old mortarman with the 1st Air Cavalry Division. Now the dean of a Bible college in California, he spends a lot of his time trying to exorcise the demons that continue to haunt so many veterans. He is a thoughtful Christian with little Christian sympathy for the hallelujah men who give preaching a bad name.

Kimball has invited us to a dinner with his men and a group of Vietcong veterans at the old Rex Hotel. The Rex was next to a building known as JUSPAO, the Joint U.S. Public Affairs Office. Reporters were briefed there every evening at five P.M. Little of value was gleaned from these briefings, which by 1970 had deteriorated to a shouting match between newly arrived correspondents and American civilian and military public affairs officers. It had become cabaret more than journalism and was aptly known as the five o'clock follies. JUSPAO is now a collection of curio shops.

I accept Kimball's invitation, and when he learns that Professor Hung is with us, he is quick to include him.

We turn up at the Rex at the appointed time and discover that there has been a change of plans. The veterans' dinner has been canceled, not by the veterans and not by their Vietnamese minder, but by a retired Vietcong colonel who magnanimously invites all of us to dinner at his house. We are told we will meet a group of Vietcong veterans who are now beginning to put their lives back together as artists, singers, musicians, and poets.

The Americans are not pleased. They had paid for the dinner in advance, and this change of plans smells badly of propaganda. But they and we have little choice but to climb into taxis and head for the colonel's villa in a distant northwestern suburb of Ho Chi Minh City.

The place is quite grand, with a strong whiff of having been "liberated"—most likely from a South Vietnamese officer who worked for the puppet régime, as they call it. One underpaid public servant inherits the spoils of another.

The colonel greets us on a stone patio that is done up as a night-club. There are some valuable bits of Cham carvings scattered around the patio and a low nightclub table; the whole set is lit in pink and purple by awful little electric lanterns. The effect is of a Midwest motel's attempt to create a Samoan piano-bar. Seated around the table are a half dozen men who have the appearance of being dragooned into this party, plus a middle-aged woman who is introduced as having been part of an entertainment troupe that performed for the fighters during the American war. There is also a young woman present, dressed in a tarty-looking sixties' Tu Do Street bar-girl outfit. A guitar is slung over her shoulder.

The colonel is roaring drunk. He is a heavy-shouldered man wearing an open white shirt, dark trousers and carrying a bottle of Ba-Muoi-ba, the local Vietnamese brew. He weaves among the veterans, spilling beer and shouting greetings and introductions, and beckons us all to sit.

Miss Mai bravely carries on a running translation of the colonel, and she is, at least to my ear and eye, doing it on automatic pilot. Miss Mai is a loyal party functionary, but she does not enjoy being the mouthpiece for this brutish man. He raves on:

"I want my American friends to meet the brave fighters whose courage defeated the expeditionary forces of the imperialists. I welcome you to listen to the songs of our revolution, and you will understand how we were victorious over the Americans and their puppet régime."

He continues for ten minutes or more. All are embarrassed; the Vietnamese quietly sip their beer. The Americans stare at the table. Professor Hung does not dare look at anyone. Finally, the colonel introduces one of his veterans. The man has one of those soft clear tenors, almost Irish in its tone. It is a lovely song, not the party paean I had expected. All about loneliness and longing and missing the girl of his dreams. Professor Hung is quite moved. It is clearly the "Hey Jude" of the other side.

It is also not the song the colonel expected, and the singer barely finishes when he orders the middle-aged woman to do the right thing with a big upbeat number about marching against the forces of imperialism. The young woman follows her with a fractured version of "Top of the World."

> Ahm on top ah de worl lookeen
> dow on keashun an de oney expanashun I ca fine,

48

is de love dat I foun evah sin you be aroun
You just pu me on de top ah de worl.

The poor thing has no voice at all. Nevertheless, she follows her attempt by explaining to us in English, French, and Vietnamese that she is the toast of Cuba and Nicaragua and would we like to hear something in Spanish. Before we can offer polite protest, the colonel interrupts and continues his harangue:

"The vile acts and atrocities of the criminal American presidents, Eisenhower, Kennedy, Johnson, and Nixon, could not defeat the progressive sentiments of our courageous men and women. Let us raise our glasses to their selfless sacrifice and their victory over the fascist war-making machine."

This crude display is typical of the propaganda ground out by Hanoi during the war. I could not understand then why they did not portray themselves, or at least most of the nation, simply as flesh-and-blood humanity that should have been spared the holocaust that was visited on them. Instead, they made themselves into the sweetest target of all, a nation of tedious sloganeering theorists.

The colonel's performance is a most unusual experience in Vietnam. I have always found people here to be, not just hospitable, but also generous in their respect for the feelings of guests. The American veterans begin to mutter to one another. The Vietnamese are uncomfortable, but noncommittal. The minders are embarrassed. The singers simply wait to go on. The colonel swigs beer and shouts slogans. The camera crew, Wade Bingham and Paul Oppenheim, records bits of this insulting performance, but mainly takes close-ups of the various guests. I ask them to turn off the camera. I do not want evidence of what I am about to say. Every instinct tells me it is wrong to do this, to become "engaged" in this way, but there comes a time when being a bystander just won't do. Watching these decent men—Americans and Vietnamese—being bullied, the time had come.

"Excuse me, sir, but will you have the good manners to allow these

49

men to talk to each other. The Americans have come a long way to try to reconcile themselves with Vietnam. You have already usurped their plans to have dinner with Vietnamese veterans. They did not come here to be lectured. Would you please have the good grace to let someone else speak."

I cannot be sure that my words have been accurately translated by the delicious Miss Mai—but from the icy hatred in the eyes of the colonel, I think she came close to the mark. Perhaps, given her Hanoi status, she went beyond it.

The Americans seem pleased by this bit of grandstanding. The Vietnamese seem pleased with the colonel's discomfort. Professor Hung looks relieved. Miss Mai smiles . . . a big nonaligned smile. The colonel flops into his chair, takes a swig from his bottle, and utters a stream of gutteral Vietnamese that is not translated, and goes silent. Unhidden contempt in his face.

The Americans rise and give their names and when and where they served. It is very formal, very touching. The room becomes a low babble of English and Vietnamese, the two minders working over-time. There are a few solemn moments, but mostly there is a strong feeling of men who survived something awful and can now even laugh about it. Hung tells of wriggling under some bushes to get away from a helicopter gunship. Somebody says, "it was probably me trying to get you."

"Deadly helicopters," says Hung.

Psychiatrists have said that it is a good thing for American veterans who are troubled by the war to return to Vietnam. It really is something remarkable, listening to these ordinary people who, a few years ago, would have blown one another away without a thought, now so curious to hear not so much their experiences as their feelings. As good as the fellowship is in this meeting, it is never boister-ous or loud. There is great formality about how these men talk together, a respect that has nothing to do with anything but a small commitment they all once shared: to do what your country asked of you.

50

Bill Baldwin, a former marine who served two tours and was wounded in Quang Tri, comes very close to tears. He is a big, bearded, soft-spoken man who is wearing a baseball cap with the legend "Vietnam Vet and Proud of It."

"I think all veterans are drawn back here," he says. "Everybody has a sense of unfinished business. I've longed for Vietnam ever since I came home. I've longed for it. I've dreamed about it. I think when I go home, the chapter will be over."

8

A Kiss Before Dying

Danang, January 21, 8:00 A.M.:   It is very strange landing in the sleepy airport at Danang, once probably the largest U.S. Marine base in the world. The only other aircraft present is a MiG-23 doing touch-and-go's. For reasons I do not understand, the Vietnamese have a customs checkpoint at Danang, even though, as far as I can tell, there are no international flights into the place. I am approached by an attractive young woman wearing enormous shoulder boards and an officer's cap with a swooping crown, the type favored by Latin American dictators. In French she asks me if I'm Russian. I explain that I am not.

"Then what are you doing here?" she asks.

I tell her we are here to talk to veterans of the American war and ask if she is police or army.

"No, I am the *douanier*," she says.

When I ask her if there is much customs work to be done in Danang, she giggles and tells me not very much. Sometimes the

Russians have things they shouldn't have. When I press her on this she does not go into details. Drugs? Dollars? She giggles at the suggestions.

When I ask her if she is from the North or the South she giggles again.

"I am from Hanoi . . . we cannot trust a Southerner to be a customs officer."

She confesses she likes it better in the South because when she is not in her ghastly uniform she can wear pretty clothes and buy lipstick, and the men in the South notice things like that.

I give the beautiful *douanier* half a dozen packs of 555 cigarettes, the English brand that is the favored smoke in Vietnam, just to see the difference in probity between Southern and Northern *douaniers*. She accepts them with a wonderful grin. In fact, 555 cigarettes are the true currency of Vietnam, more acceptable to most people than the near valueless dong.

We drive north to Hue along the coast and through the Hai Ban mountain pass. The most remarkable thing about Vietnam at peace is the ability to use the roads. I have made this trip before but only by helicopter. I remember what a spectacular-looking country this is. Perhaps not worth the millions of lives spent in winning it, but certainly a place worth fighting for. Up here the South China Sea is to your right and, ahead and to the left, the misty mountains. Only a few fishing villages are along the coast, each with its acres of nets drying on poles. There is up here a timelessness that assaults you in the most benign kind of way. After the grasping, choking atmosphere of Thailand, Vietnam comes as a welcome pause. There is a serenity here that is made up of equal parts of poverty, introspection, and, I believe, the strongest sense of identity, of relationship with the land that you will find anywhere. It is almost patriotism as faith.

Thailand, by contrast, seems morally and spiritually bankrupt. The place became very rich off the Vietnam War, and now in peace it seems to get even richer off Vietnam's isolation. With its wealth it

53

has turned Bangkok into the ugliest city in Asia. It is a jerry-built bazaar, a tourist-mill that denies the visitor the right of strangeness. It has turned its faith into a Disneyland attraction and its culture into an Atlantic City casino show. It has killed its forests and turned the glorious Mekong into an industrial sewer. It sits in squalid prosperity to Vietnam's west, an overstuffed pasha gloating over his neighbor's misfortune.

I muse on these contrasts as we drive through miles of unbulldozed coastline. Whatever the war did to the terrain, nature quickly undid. In places you still find B-52 bomb craters, but they've been turned into irrigation reservoirs and fish ponds.

I will not get to Khe Sanh on this trip. The little valley up in the northwest corner of Vietnam was the site of one of the largest bloodlettings of the war. I am told that Khe Sanh is still claiming lives with its rich supply of land mines and unexploded artillery shells. I have a friend who was in the OSS in the late forties, and he used to go tiger hunting in the valley of Khe Sanh with rich Frenchmen from Danang, then called Tourane. I feel quite safe in these tidy little pastoral thoughts.

Still, I expect if Vietnam does open up to the West, which it wants to do desperately, the Vietnamese will make most of the same mistakes as the Thais. One hopes that the sense of land as a borrowed asset that must be passed on intact will protect them from the worst excesses of their Asian neighbors. Having to "do" something with real estate, raging Trumpism, is a seductive and infectious ideology that even the steely character of these people may be too weak to resist.

We arrive in Hue just before dusk. Our only appointment today is with five retired officers. The meeting place is their club, the former palace of the mother of Bao Dai, the emperor of Vietnam who abdicated in 1945. He lives in the south of France, a pitiful footnote to history who attends galas for the comte de Paris and the other great pretenders to the thrones of Europe.

Morley Safer

They tell me that Bao Dai's mother, the dowager empress, gave her palace to the veterans in 1975. I am sure this aged woman had little choice in the matter, but whether this "gift" is propaganda or not, it makes for a romantic story and fits in nicely with the Vietnamese tradition of glorifying the courage and nobility of women.

After all, it was the Trung sisters who started the whole affair almost two thousand years ago. The two sisters led an uprising that overwhelmed the Chinese occupiers. Four years later the Chinese crushed the revolt, and the sisters chose suicide by drowning in the River Day over surrender. The sisters are celebrated by all Vietnamese, and I doubt if a day goes by in this country that a play is not performed reminding one and all of this militant feminine heritage. The sisters were the first "fighters" and in a sense the first Vietnamese, the twin mothers of all who came after.

I am curious about the clubhouse. The mother of a dear friend lived here most of her life. She was a lady-in-waiting to the empress, and I remember long descriptions by my friend, Ha Thuc Can, of his mother's life in this house. Can was a brilliant cameraman during the war, but by the early seventies he was exhausted by the work and by New York's demands for more and more combat footage, and by a series of young "unblooded" correspondents who kept arriving in Vietnam. Can saw little value in winning an Overseas Press Club Award, posthumously. Because he hadn't worked for CBS for a couple of years, he was denied a place on the plane the company chartered to evacuate Vietnamese personnel and their families from Saigon.

On April 27, 1975, just three days before Saigon fell, he called me in New York. He was desperate. I called the foreign desk and the Saigon bureau and was told that every seat had been spoken for. Ha Thuc Can would have to find his own way out. Next I called the State Department in Washington. Can had friends there, people he'd helped in the early sixties. I was told there was an outside chance they could get him on the plane, but he would have to stay by his phone twenty-four hours a day—not use it—and wait for a call, and when it came he must move instantly. But there were no guarantees the call would come.

"If he has to stay by his phone and not use it, how on earth will he be able to get out of the country if your call doesn't come?"

"That's up to him . . . he has to make that decision," I was told.

I called him in Saigon with the disheartening news and suggested he go immediately to the bureau with his wife and two infant children and *force* themselves into the evacuation.

"There are plenty of people there who know you, correspondents, producers. Hell, you introduced most of the Vietnamese cameramen and soundmen to CBS. You hired practically the whole staff. Surely, they'll make room for you."

"They have their own problems. They're trying to get their mothers and cousins out. Besides, you know me, Morley. You know I'd rather die than beg."

Indeed I knew.

"Good-bye, Can. Good luck. I'll keep trying to put heat on the State Department."

Can and his family did get out, a day later, without the help of either CBS or the State Department. Peter Arnett, who it seemed had been in Vietnam forever for the Associated Press, finessed the family's escape.

Arnett, a New Zealander who now works for CNN in Washington, was probably the toughest, fairest, most consistent of all the hundreds of reporters who covered the war. He is a feisty but modest man with the face of a boxer who'd taken as much as he'd given. Above all, he is a magnificent friend.

I heard the story of Arnett's efforts years later from Ha Thuc Can.

"Just after I talked to you in New York on the twenty-seventh, Peter came by and told me he would try to get me on the AP plane.

"The next morning, the twenty-eighth, he was in front of the apartment in a jeep. The four of us climbed in, and my wife said I should go back and get my cameras and other valuables. 'No,' I said,

56

'just us.' The only thing we took was a big box of Klim, the powdered milk. It was the only food the youngest baby would take. We drove to the airport, but the guards would not let us through. Three more times, Peter drove us back to Saigon, where we changed cars, and came back to the airport, and each time we were turned away. Finally, the last time, in the last car we could find, we just burst through the gate and drove to the hangar. I thought for sure the guards would open up on us, that the four of us and Peter would never leave Vietnam alive."

Typically, Arnett stayed on in Saigon after the fall, one of the few Western journalists to take the risk. A month or so later he was thrown out of the country.

Ha Thuc Can, who fifteen years ago arrived penniless in the Philippines, with three dependents and a box of Klim, is now a successful art dealer with galleries in Hong Kong and Singapore. He commutes regularly to Vietnam and has written a book on the archaeology of the country.

The palace his mother lived in with the dowager empress is a magnificent small building. A grand staircase leads up to enormous doors and into a mahogany and teak salon. The walls are covered in gilt and teak paneling with more Chinese giltwork on the heavy frames of paintings of nineteenth-century Vietnamese life. The palace has been kept immaculate, and I wonder why. It is not important enough to be a tourist attraction. If the tourists ever do descend on Hue there is plenty more to see in the Citadel and on boat trips on the Perfume River. I suspect the reason is a genuine respect for what came before. At the same time they are extremely practical about their historic sites. They use them; they do not worship them or, as the Soviets and Chinese have done, turn them into showpiece examples of the decadence that preceded the revolution. The Vietnamese would regard such displays as silly boastfulness and as a denial of their heritage. So part of this lovely villa is used as a youth club and part as a club for retired officers.

The officers troop in at dusk, five men in their sixties, big men for

57

Vietnamese, straight-backed but extremely slow of foot. Tea is served, and they are eager to talk . . . not so much about the war as about why we are so interested in the war. Again, the American war is regarded here, especially by old men like these, as a mere episode. All of them are veterans of the French war, and two of them fought at Dien Bien Phu. They agree that, of the two, the American war was the most vicious, "the most cruel," they say. They talk of B-52s, and it is clear enough that it was the B-52 strikes that generate these bitter memories. Everywhere in Vietnam when people talk of the war, these high-altitude, remote, and impersonal attacks are recalled with remarkable clarity. Each person has his own B-52 story.

Colonel Nguyen Ngoc Hoa was the commander of Transport Unit 559, an army group renowned throughout Vietnam. It is regarded with the kind of respect and affection that the American people had for the marines or the Rangers in the Second World War. Hauling supplies down the Ho Chi Minh Trail was the essential tactic of this war, so a transport unit, which other nations might dismiss as the mundane but necessary backdrop to the high adventures of, say, a parachute brigade, became the legendary outfit that makes the difference between defeat and victory.

Colonel Hoa's daily menace was the B-52. Whether they came or not, the fear of an interdiction attack on his supply routes had its effect on his men. It made a very slow and laborious journey even slower. Colonel Hoa says that he has many bad memories of the war, of losing close friends, of seeing what devastation a bombing attack can bring to a unit. "We carried so much, so far, and then we see it turn to dust in an instant."

I ask him if he was jealous of the Americans and their airplanes and helicopters.

"Yes, I was jealous every day, especially of the C-130s, the big transport planes, and the Chinook helicopters. The Americans could move more supplies and men in an hour than I could move in a month. But you see it made no difference in the end. I think we understood our limitations better than you understood your advantages."

58

His worst memory was of seeing a woman whose legs had been cut off by bomb shrapnel. "She was lying in a road still alive. She was beyond pain, but she knew she was going to die, and I knew there was nothing I could do for her. She asked me to kiss her before she died. I did. I will never forget her."

Colonel Huang Dai Hai commanded an artillery and antiaircraft unit. He says it was his outfit that shot down an American pilot named Shumaker.* He never met Shumaker formally but saw him when he was captured. "Please send Shumaker my greetings. If he ever comes to Vietnam, I would like to invite him to come to my house. In war we were enemies, but now we have peace and why can we not be friends?"

Colonel Hai's greatest regret about the war is that he never married. "I didn't want to have someone suffer if I died. It was a mistake. I should have married . . . but if there is a woman anywhere in the world who will marry me, with my silver hair, I will accept her."

The colonel smiles at this, and his buddies needle him good-naturedly.

The worst of it for him was seeing eighteen-year-olds, fresh from secondary school: "They would receive one month of training, and the next month they would be in battle. Their first battle, and they would not come back. I still remember their faces, and I still write to their families. I consider those young people my nieces and nephews, my brothers and sisters. I don't want to call them my children because I never married, but they could have been my children.

"When you join the army you take seven oaths, the seventh is to swear to live together, die together, and share sorrows as if they were joys. I still maintain that oath, even now . . . but I have feelings of guilt . . . I feel it was my fault that we didn't win this war more

*Retired Admiral Robert Shumaker was a lieutenant commander when he was shot down over North Vietnam in February 1965. He was the second American POW. He spent eight years in prison camp, where he showed great courage and fortitude. He was tortured, he says, and spent three years in solitary confinement. "One cell mate was beaten to death. I don't remember Colonel Hai, and I am not so sure I want to meet him either."

59

quickly. But I must be very frank with you and tell you that, even though we now want reconciliation with the United States and I agree with that official policy, I still hate those people who thrust war upon our country and those people who committed crimes in our country. I am now an old man alone, and that war made my life like this. I joined the army when I was seventeen. When I retired my hair turned white. I have not had a normal life. I blame the Americans for this."

Miss Mai seems both touched and annoyed with Colonel Hai's remarks. This lonely old soldier, this "uncle" of so many dead children, is not supposed to say he hates Americans. "Hated" is acceptable; "hates" violates the current policy of reconciliation. She mutters something to him in Vietnamese, a brief scolding. The other colonels nod their approval, but silvery-headed old Hai simply stares into the distance. Mai repeatedly had the opportunity to mistranslate to conform to Hanoi's policy, but something in her, perhaps her devout belief in accuracy and precision of language, prevents her. She seems to prefer to translate accurately then give the culprit a tough reminder about who's in charge.

Electricity seems to be a problem in Hue. Throughout the interview the lights go off, come back on in ten minutes, and then we are in darkness again ten minutes later.

Finally, at nine o'clock, the lights go out for good, and we have to pick our way out of the palace by the glow of cigarette lighters and matches. When I inquire about these power cuts—one half of Hue was glowing bright, our half was in total darkness—I am told by an extremely officious representative of the mayor who sat in on the interview that there was an internal party squabble and that sometimes it was necessary to remind certain factions in Hue who had the real power. "Also," he said, "there is a shortage of electricity."

9

The Land of Fairies and Dragons

In the spring of 1968 the gates and walls of the Citadel in Hue were as familiar to Americans as their living-room furniture. The stout walls and squat bastions, the stacks of North Vietnamese dead, and the wounded marines made it, for a few days, a kind of Alamo for both sides. A steel-helmeted, flak-jacketed Walter Cronkite confirmed to the American people, and, as it turned out, to Lyndon Johnson, that the battle for Hue was no mere incident.

The war was over at Hue. The United States had won the battle, but the experience had exhausted Lyndon Johnson and the American people as well. Weeks after the battle he announced he would not be a candidate for reelection. The war was over at Hue . . . it just took seven more years and a few hundred thousand corpses to confirm it.

American marines fought a very good fight at Hue. They lost one hundred fifty men. The North lost five thousand or more. When the marines were finished mopping up they found the awful evidence of massacre. God only knows how many civilians the men from the North had slaughtered. It seemed they had simply gone on a binge of killing. But later, when the bodies were uncovered, it was clear that the victims—hundreds of them—had been carefully selected.

I walk along the ramparts of Hue looking for the scars of the siege. Not much is visible. Ruins can take a terrible battering and not show it. The pockmarks of bullets and the deeper wounds of mortar rounds give the ancient granite texture, and nature does a fine job of fooling the eye. The ravages of age and the assaults of men are softened by the same fine fuzz of Asian mildew.

Hue was and is a recalcitrant place. It is still the center of thought in Vietnam, but not the way that might be said of Oxford or Cambridge or other great university cities. Unlike the others, Hue with its imperial splendor has become the bricks-and-mortar representation of a nation's character. When French missionaries tried conversion on Hue at the end of the eighteenth century, they found it necessary to slaughter or be slaughtered.

What is called Buddhism here is really a representation of "Vietnamese-ness." The Buddhism of the center of Vietnam includes Confucianism with its practical ideas about justice, loyalty, and the state, and incorporates the glorious mystical abstractions in the teachings of Lao-tzu and the Taoists. Revered bonzes and distinguished professors of medicine speak in the same language of militant nationalism. University lectures are interchangeable with temple sermons. If American policy in Indochina had been based on even a cursory reading of Vietnamese history, it would have been clear that, in one way or another, in one form or another, this beautiful unlucky land would rid itself of foreigners once and for all. At the turn of the century, Phan Boi Chau, a Nationalist in exile in China, smuggled in a pamphlet called "New Letters Written in Blood." The nationalist tract inflamed the students of Hue. He followed it with the works of Rousseau, Voltaire, Diderot, and Montesquieu, turning the works of France's most respected thinkers into fuel for the fire that would

62

destroy France in Indochina. The flame never went out, and it burned with a white heat in Hue.

Something else was happening in Hue. The old resistance to modernism had given way to an acceptance of foreign education and literature, especially foreign ideas like "The Rights of Man." But unlike most movements toward progressive ideas, it did not reject the past. History and what can only be described as faith in themselves are the red and white corpuscles of the Vietnamese. Letters, quite literally, "written in blood."

In the early sixties the State Department received a letter, a plea really, from a group of Hue intellectuals calling on the U.S. government to cease giving aid to the fanatically Catholic régime of Diem . . . that the aid was helping to crush Buddhism . . . that the Vietnamese people were and will continue to be the people of *Tien Rong*—the people of "Fairies and Dragons."

The letter could have served as a warning that men and women who maintain a spiritual connection with ancestors who lived four thousand years ago have a certain strength that may not be easily softened or seduced by napalm or goodwill.

Walking along the ramparts on this freezing January morning, I wonder about the reaction to that letter from Hue. Was it simply that the old Asia hands in Washington could more easily accept the Immaculate Conception and the Resurrection than they could Fairies and Dragons?

It is a long drive from Hue to Quang Tri City, long and quite treacherous. The car, whose make or age I cannot fathom, is equipped, curiously, with right-hand drive. The tires are quite bald, which makes stopping in this relentless rain a giddy adventure in brake-lock. But the driver, Mr. Bai, is more than capable. He is a man in his late twenties who speaks not a word of English but seems to have a complete understanding of the language. He chain-smokes duty-free 555s with one hand and with the other digs into a bag of Hershey bars I brought along. Elbows and forearms do the steering.

63

He is meticulous about his car, less so about the byways of Vietnam. With three Olympian smokers in the car, myself, himself, and Patti Hassler, he makes regular stops to empty ashtrays. The third passenger is Professor Hung. We are taking him to Quang Tri, where he was in the thick of the fighting in 1972.

The war in this northern neck of South Vietnam was much more conventional than anything fought previously. Both sides had heavy artillery and tanks, with the South Vietnamese supported by American aircraft.

The tenacity of the North Vietnamese and Vietcong has given them a reputation of being invincible in battle. As we slosh north along Highway 9, Professor Hung tells tales that reduce these men to mortals. Or at the very least, they join that stalwart and awkward International Brigade of draftees who might engage in more useful combat had they been left home to roll bandages.

An American 25th Infantry Division major once described to me his allotment of graduate-student draftees: "We took them up to the Cambodian border, and all they did was step on their own dinguses."

Professor Hung's version of stepping on his own dingus occurred in the battle of Quang Tri. He was Sergeant Hung, and he was commanding a squad of men guarding a road.

"One of our tanks approached us," he recalls. "I mean, we thought it was our tank because it was flying our flag from its aerial. But suddenly it started shooting at us. We took some casualties.

"There had been rumors of South Vietnamese tanks infiltrating our lines by flying captured flags. The next day we saw three tanks approaching, all flying our flag. We had a B-40 rocket launcher, and we got the first one . . . and then we got the second one, and the third one stopped and backed up into the forest. We followed it in and we saw a bunch of soldiers cooking rice over a fire. The men in the third tank jumped out and ran away when they saw us, and that made the soldiers who were cooking run away too. Then we got the third tank and it blew up. We were very pleased with ourselves . . . until we realized we'd just destroyed three of our own tanks.

64

Morley Safer

Nobody said a word . . . we just quietly withdrew back to the road."

Halfway to Quang Tri City the left rear tire gives out, and the car does an extraordinary ballet movement using the entire width of Highway 1. Mr. Bai, the driver, is not panicked for a moment. He goes with the skid nicely and makes a landing and full stop that Baryshnikov would have been proud of. He insists on changing the tire alone, and the three of us take shelter from the rain under a bamboo awning set against a small cement-block cottage near the road. In seconds children are squealing around us, and their mother beckons us in. Tea and cakes are produced. The inevitable granny oversees the presentation with chatty disapproval. A born mother-in-law, this woman. I am in the dark as to what she is saying, but the gist is clear: "Why haven't you made *fresh* tea for these travelers? That cup the stone-faced one is drinking from is cracked!"

The hospitality of ordinary Vietnamese who one meets in this accidental manner is wrenching. They are so poor yet so anxious to share what they have, get so much pleasure from giving the small gift of tea and cakes to strangers. Their lives seem bleak to eyes that judge contentment by the measure of leisure time and the consumer price index. The Vietnamese may take their pleasures in tiny ways, but they do not take them sadly.

Beyond the faded photograph of a grandfather and a small altar, the room is free of decoration. The walls have been given a wash of ocher glaze that a New York decorator would, as they say, "die for." There are half a dozen beds in the room, with a bamboo screen that offers only a minimum of privacy around the one that belongs to the owner and his wife.

Through Hung, the woman explains that her husband is away at work. He drives a truck for a local agricultural cooperative. I have seen these trucks. They are mostly worn-out former military transports that are kept running in the most ingenious ways. The first vital organ to give in to rust, always, is the radiator. This is kept functioning by mounting a fifty-five-gallon drum of water on the roof of the cab and running a piece of garden hose down into the radiator.

65

Enough water gets pumped through the system to keep the engine cool, before it finds its way out through the leaky bottom. Every ten or fifteen miles on every road in Vietnam there is a filling station, a place to top up the drum with water.

We thank the family for their kindness and go on our way. Hung is quite shaken as we pull into the southern suburbs of Quang Tri. That awful battle could have taken place a week ago, not seventeen years ago. Both sides of the highway are littered with shot-up tanks and broken artillery pieces, and the buildings have had their faces shot off. After all these years of abandonment, one still feels slightly embarrassed, slightly nosy, peering this way into someone's privacy. The buildings are tilted crazily. Has the central government pur- posely left them standing so precariously as bitter monuments, or is it just too poor to do anything about it? I suspect it is the latter. Apart from the cemeteries everywhere, they do not make much of the war.

Hung fought here in the battle for Quang Tri. He had a cousin who was with the puppet army of Saigon, he tells me.

"He was here in Quang Tri when we came across the river at the beginning of that campaign. I met him in Ho Chi Minh City last year. We found it very difficult to even look at each other."

Hung and I leave the car and walk down to the east bank of the Thach Han River. It is a quarter of a mile wide at this point—a swift-flowing muddy stream that Hung and his unit plus an entire division crossed over in a day and a night in 1972.

"We sent frogmen over the first night," he says. "They had cables with them that they secured on this side. Then we followed, pulling ourselves across, hand over hand."

The fighting here was almost entirely between Vietnamese. It was at the height of what Americans called "Vietnamization of the war," and Hanoi called the "de-Americanization."

I ask Hung, as we walk along the muddy bank, if they ever heard any war news.

66

"We had radios," he says. "It was forbidden to listen to the stations in the South. At night we would listen to the news from Hanoi. Of course it always reported victories . . . and the student demonstrations in the United States were all reported in great detail. I know the names of the American universities just from listening to the war news. Radio Hanoi also reported the cruelty of American soldiers and how cowardly they were."

"Cruelty?"

"Yes, cutting the ears off the dead; I remember that report."

I tell Hung that the story of the ears was first reported on CBS News, not by me, but by another correspondent.

He seems puzzled by this bit of confirmation. "Then it's true? They did cut the ears off our soldiers?"

I explain that there were incidents of brutality. That this was not a policy. That something happens to ordinary men during and after battle. That for the most part American soldiers were decent men who did what was asked of them.

"I never fought against the Americans," Hung says. "But people who did told me they would try to avoid hand-to-hand fighting. They would withdraw and call in artillery. My friends who fought against Americans thought they were well trained and well disciplined but had no stomach for battle . . . they said they were weak."

My mind drifts to a dozen acts of supreme courage that I had witnessed in Vietnam, of the tenderness shown by fearsome-looking men to village children whose older brothers had planted mines and booby traps. I remember one black sergeant, an enormous man, who had himself been raised in the most appalling conditions in Chicago, dancing across a dike during a mortar attack and pulling two children to safety.

I am not in a mood to debate with Hung the comparative valor of Americans and Vietnamese; apparently, neither is he. We both feel slightly embarrassed that the subject came up. Most of what both sides heard about each other were lies anyway.

67

10

"The Birds Still Sang"

3:00 P.M.:   We continue the drive north from Quang Tri practically to the old DMZ and then turn off onto an unpaved track, heading for the Trung Son Cemetery. This is as poor a part of Vietnam as I have seen. The houses are made of sticks splattered with mud. The land is a sweeping unproductive plateau. Here and there are a few vegetable gardens; otherwise it is rocky, bony soil where, beyond some stunted trees, nothing else is growing. This is not the Vietnam of the lush deltas and rich coastal plain.

This part of South Vietnam was doused with a monsoon of defoliants. It is impossible for me to tell if this barren plain is the result of nature or the research and development of Dow Chemical and Monsanto, manufacturers of Agent Orange and other useful products. Other firms made Agent Orange as well. Among them, a company with the horrifying name of Thompson-Hayward, Nutrition and Agriculture.

It was chemical warfare pure and simple. Its defenders had the arrogance to maintain that what would kill trees would not hurt people, or American people anyway. We knew it was dirty work from the beginning. An officer confessed it to a friend in 1964, before we were supposed to be using it.

The Vietnamese in these parts tell me that the area around Quang Tri is the most traumatized in all of Vietnam. Beyond the battering it took from the artillery of three armies, the B-52 raids, the regular bombing and strafing of South Vietnamese and American fighter-bombers, there is the legacy of Agent Orange—the poisoned land, the various cancers, the birth defects.

The American servicemen who share the legacy have sued their government. These people have no one to sue. They do not even complain very much. There is no one to complain to. They can only scratch at this unforgiving land for less than enough to eat.

We pass families gathering firewood. Even the smallest among them has an enormous load on his back. All of them, of course, are barefoot on this freezing, wet January day. Hung had asked me earlier what was the most precious thing when I was out on operations in the mud. "Socks," I said, "dry socks." He'd laughed. "We never had to worry about socks."

We drive through the gates of Trung Son Cemetery and stop at the administration building. It is a bare room except for a gold bust of Ho Chi Minh and a few small tables, each one bearing a thick ledger, the kind bookkeepers use. The ledgers contain the names, hometowns, and death dates of ten thousand men and women buried at Trung Son. Hung's face has grown very pale. He is looking for two names, those of his brother and his closest friend. He knows it is extremely unlikely he will find either name, either grave. He has no idea when or where his brother was killed; as for his friend, he'd buried him himself, somewhere along the Laotian border. Still, he hopes that somehow both might have been found and reburied in this Cemetery of Honor.

Hung goes through all the ledgers twice but finds neither name.

69

There are eighty steps up to the burial ground. The effect of this is to reveal slowly the extent of the place. Not until the final step is reached does one realize that the graves stretch in every direction to the horizon. They are in rows that have been planted in perfectly straight lines. The effect is the same at Arlington or Verdun or St. Laurent-sur-Mer in Normandy. A quarter turn of the head and the eyes catch another perfect row that seems endless. There is the same small blow to the heart, as well. Their youth of course is what does it. The effect on Hung is devastating. He cannot talk for minutes. Then he says, "I have never seen so many in one place. Ten thousand, ten thousand of my family. They were the best sons and daughters of Vietnam."

The effect of his words are as chilling as this place. Years ago I was having a badly needed drink on the terrace of a hotel in Normandy. I had just returned from the cemetery at St. Laurent-sur-Mer, where most of the American casualties suffered at Omaha Beach lay buried. At the next table was a man in his late fifties. He was a veteran of D-Day who made a pilgrimage every year to the cemetery.

"They are like my brothers, you know . . . brothers who never grew old. They were the best sons our country had."

My daughter, who was thirteen at the time, had walked through the cemetery that day with a look of tragic bafflement on her face. She was confronting, perhaps for the first time, or at least in the most powerful way possible, the illogic of death in youth. When she asked "Why?" over and over again, it was not the "Why?" of a child.

The graves at Trung Son are small cement-covered mounds with a Gothic-arched headstone bearing each soldier's name, age, and birthplace. Here and there the markers have fallen over. As we walk along, Hung forces them back into place, firmly but with great tenderness . . . patting each of them when he completes the work. The conversation turns yet again to the B-52 raids. Hung looks up at the overcast sky in this utterly silent place.

"You always knew when the B-52s were coming . . . when the

observation and reconnaissance planes would leave, there was silence—except the birds still sang. There was nothing you could do but stare up at the sky and wait. That was it. You knew it was over when the last bomb exploded and you were still alive. In 1972 the B-52s were coming all day, in succession . . . and from Hue to Quang Tri, especially in Quang Tri, you could see nothing at all. The dust was so thick it was as if it was night."

"Did many people desert? Many who could just not take it anymore?"

"In my unit we had some. One soldier, who was terribly brave. One day he came back from an attack and told me about the killing, and that night he had a terrible nightmare about it. The next day he could not eat. He told me that when he looked at the meat he imagined it was human meat, and then he deserted. He was really a very brave man. If he'd stayed, he would have got a medal. But I can't say that I blame him."

Hung's graphic, painful description somehow makes desertion less grievous. On this overcast day, scanning this endless vista of death markers, desertion seems a logical response. Siegfried Sassoon's lovely poem "Dreamers"—"Soldiers are citizens of death's grey land, drawing no dividend from time's tomorrows"—has been running through my head in this place. I think of Bill Baldwin, one of the "vets with a mission," talking about the death of a friend, through sobs he could barely control: ". . . and that morning he was shot by a sniper in the stomach and he was right beside me and it took him fifteen minutes to die. And the shock has never left me. And I can't remember his name . . . and it really bothers me . . . and it's been twenty years . . . and I can't remember his name. I can't remember his name."

The survivors, Bill Baldwin, Nguyen Ngoc Hung, have drawn their dividends, and they are ugly and profitless.

I ask Hung about his friend, how he died.

"What is there to tell? We buried him, or most of him. All I can

71

tell you is that I cried. I cried a lot. When I got back after the war, I went to see his family to tell them the day he died and that we buried him. I went to see them again last year. They will never recover."

There is a tower, a memorial, at the entrance to Trung Son; it bears the legend:

To

QUOC

GHI

CONG

"The Nation Honors Its Glorious Dead"

At the bottom of the inscription is an altar filled to overflowing with ashes. Hung has brought joss sticks with him, the burned offering for the dead. He climbs the steps to the altar and lays the burning sticks among the ashes. His hands drift through the smoke, and he makes a silent prayer. His face is the color of ashes.

As we walk back to the car Hung repeats something he'd said to me in Hanoi, something quite fitting amid these ten thousand graves. Then I had asked him who had won the war. This time I didn't ask; he just spoke, almost thinking out loud.

"At first we thought we won the war . . . but I look at this place and I realize we did not. It was something like fighting with some-body in your house with all the precious furniture around you. And after the stranger leaves, you look at the different things in your house. And they are all broken. The war actually took place in our house. It was a very sad thing. Think about it . . . after all that war, we haven't been able to change you, and you haven't been able to change us."

It is almost dark as we begin the long haul back to Danang. It will be a rough one—driving at night in the wet through the Hai Ban mountain pass. Hung's words linger. I recall a dinner at the Plaza

72

Hotel in New York at Christmas 1965. I had come back to take part, with other CBS News correspondents, in one of those awful year-end review dog-and-pony shows. My companion was James Cameron, the British journalist who had just returned from Hanoi and who'd made quite a splash as the first Western journalist of any renown to be let into the place.

I had been grilling him about the North, about the American air strikes he had witnessed, about the view of the South from Hanoi.

"You know," he said, "the worst thing this war has done? It has corrupted a tranquil Asian atmosphere into a kind of contest of beastliness. It just should not have happened where it happened. The Vietnamese are the most cultivated people in the world. Western countries have an imperfect notion of the nature of what they call "communism" in Asia. There should be another, less emotive word for it. Outside of the jargon-talkers and the official cadres, you have to search very hard in Hanoi to find a doctrinaire Marxist. Whatever Asian communism is, it is a special product of a peasant society. In Vietnam for the first time in God knows how long, they have found a movement that caters not only to their hopes, but to their needs. I hate to say this, but in Hanoi they believe the Americans would rather kill them than let them vote."

These thoughts of twenty-four years ago make me almost pleased that we are driving back in the dark. I will not have to witness, for the second time this day, the evidence in Hue and Quang Tri of Cameron's "contest of beastliness."

11

"Give Bobby My Best"

Danang, January 23, 6:00 A.M.: At breakfast in the cavernous dining room of the Phuong Dong Hotel in Danang, there is a bleary-eyed, slightly hungover contingent of foreigners. Apart from the Japanese and Australian hawkers of fish-processing plants, there is a survey crew for a Belgian television company. Its leader is a noisy young man trying his best, and succeeding, at looking like a mercenary in the Congo wars of the early sixties. He could not have been born when "Mad Mike" Hoare and his army of Belgian and British castaways were terrorizing, among other places, the Memling Hotel in Léopoldville, but he performs brilliantly. The Congo is now Zaire, and Léopoldville is now Kinshasa, but here in front of me the decorum of the Memling lives on.

The young Belgian's head is shaved, and he is wearing a beautifully controlled three-day growth of beard, a greasy T-shirt, and baggy army trousers with more pockets on their terrain than the most overprepared soldier could possibly use. He is bottomed-off with high-top paratrooper's boots. Where once there would have been a 9 mm Browning automatic shoved between belly and belt, there is a light meter. This rather benign touch makes him seem more ludicrous than brutish. But he does his best, shouting at waiters in coarse French, demanding more beer and coffee for his breakfast. The waiters—virtually none of whom speak French—glide by as if he did not exist. He is altogether a pushy bugger who is running a great risk of giving Belgians a reputation for crudeness.

Our table includes the CBS caravan, plus Professor Hung; cute-as-a-button Miss Mai, chief minder and terrifier-of-veterans of two wars; and Mr. Ming, a local Danang minder. David Greenway of *The Boston Globe* and his wife J.B'. have joined us for breakfast. Greenway, who has served sentences in Southeast Asia and Beirut for *Time* and *The Washington Post*, has now settled into a bucolic and less stressful life as a columnist and assistant to the editor of *The Boston Globe.* He and his wife are touring Vietnam, retracing David's footsteps. He was almost killed during the battle of Hue and was later decorated by the marines. It's funny how we are fascinated by the places where we came near to losing our lives. It's something like visiting one's own tombstone. David and Hung are at one end of the table, deep in conversation. Both fine men; both calm enthusiasts.

At my end I am discussing with Miss Mai aspects of Vietnamese and American culture.

"I envy Americans, especially American women; they can do anything they want, even have a baby without marrying the guy. If that happened in Vietnam, the woman wouldn't even be able to get a job."

"You mean the government would disapprove?"

"Ha! Whatever the government is, we are still very formal people, very moral, at least in the North. I honestly like it that way; it makes me feel secure, but what the hell, I would like to be able to take some risks too."

She confesses that more than anything she would like to study in

Flashbacks

the United States. Some Vietnamese have been able to get scholarships. I avoid asking her if she would consider staying if she was lucky enough to get permission to go abroad. She has already said she feels an obligation to her country, and I'm afraid if I raise the question she will clam up. This is the first unguarded conversation we have had, although she and Patti Hassler have become very close, very much the easy relationship of modern professional women.

I suspect Miss Mai is under the illusion that Western women really "have it all," given the fact that the only Westerners she meets, men or women, seem to lead such unburdened lives. People who seem able to put everything—physical, emotional, spiritual—on an American Express Gold Card that never needs repayment. People whose lives seemingly can be contained in one suitcase, a carry-on bag, and a small piece of plastic.

Miss Mai is due to be married in Hanoi after we leave.

"I am getting dangerously close to thirty," she tells me. "And for a Vietnamese woman, if you're not married by thirty, it's all over."

The engagement followed the strict rules of traditional Vietnamese behavior, which she explains:

"I bring the boy home to meet my parents. If they approve, I then invite him again with his parents. If they approve again, then I invite them home for a third time, during which presents are exchanged, and we are officially engaged. The big problem is where to live. My family has a big house, and I have practically the entire second floor to myself. My mother came from an aristocratic family, and my father was a poor farmer, but a very clever one. He has a good job with the government.

"My fiancé's family lives in a two-room apartment, and tradition dictates that we move in with them. This is one tradition I can do without. We still have to work it out. I don't see myself living in one room, or part of one room, with a lot of other people."

The mood at breakfast is very jolly, a reaction perhaps to the grimness of the previous day at Trung Son Cemetery.

76

I ask Miss Mai if she and the other minders have engaged in that deliciously mean-spirited Vietnamese habit of nicknaming foreigners, and if so, what are the tags put on us—on the CBS troupe. She blushes slightly and lets out an enormous whoop of laughter.

"I'll never tell," she says.

I persist. "Come on, I won't be offended. When I was in Saigon the Vietnamese in the bureau called me 'Stone Face' behind my back."

She smiles at this, says, "Not bad," but refuses to divulge her secret.

I am pleased that the traditional stiffness of the North overlaid with the Calvinism of Vietnamese communism has not stifled the zest in this lively young woman.

Breakfast arrives, fresh fruit, eggs, rice with vegetables, and wonderfully strong coffee. The French bread they serve is as crisp and rich as you will find anywhere in Provence. There are some virtues in the legacy of French colonialism. Food mostly . . . a nice exchange of cuisines, such delicacies as white asparagus in Dalat, a *crémerie* in Saigon. There was a shop on Nguyen Hue Street in Saigon that used to sell canned Beaujolais. It was a heavy but necessary addition to the backpacks of at least a few correspondents. With the wine and a couple of cans of C ration beef stew, you could make a passable boeuf bourguignon, provided you remembered a pepper mill and some garlic. The most important ingredient was a pinch or two of C-4 plastic explosive. When touched with a match, the C-4 does not explode; it burns with an intensity that brings a can of C rations to a boil in seconds. It was the microwave of its day.

These thoughts of French legacy set me to wondering what the best remnant of the American visitation might be, now almost twenty years since Richard Nixon decided that the Vietnam War should be "Vietnamized." I can think of nothing but the round-eyed beige-skinned children, now adolescents, who mill around the places visited by foreigners. The truly damned of Vietnam. I cannot even think of anything funny. Uncle Ho smoked Kools and then Salems . . . but he imported them long before the Americans came. The clap was here before Young America came to catch it . . . there are, of course, a few mine fields still maiming even the most wary of peasants.

Mr. Ming, the Danang minder, breaks the reverie to tell us we must finish our breakfast and get moving. He is a small, wiry man extremely eager to please, extremely eager to prove to everyone—especially Miss Mai—that the Danang bureau is a treasure of efficiency.

Mr. Ming has a smile that does not quit. He is a master of the two-handed handshake, which he offers up even if he is going for a pee.

He is getting very nervous, fearful that Miss Mai will turn him in on a charge of sloppy scheduling. We take the time anyway to say our farewells to Nguyen Ngoc Hung, who has joined us. He will be returning to Hanoi this morning. We heap more gifts on him, a copy of Sheehan's *Bright Shining Lie*, all my spare paperbacks, a copy of *Travels in Indo-China*, the diary of Henri Mouhot, the explorer sent out by various British scientific societies in the 1850s. Hung, I am sure, will be amused to discover how civilly and occasionally savagely his ancestors treated learned gentlemen from Europe. I also give him presents for his sons, digital watches bought from street vendors in Bangkok.

Hung's wistful ballerina's face is sadder than ever. I think he is genuinely going to miss us. To be able to sit and idly chatter on in English about things other than the war . . . children, schools, the easy banter generated by long, uncomfortable motor trips has been a great treat for him. There is more than a twinge of emotion as he leaves for the airport, everyone promising to write and send books, videos, magazines. I do not think I know a better man, more thoughtful, more civilized than Professor Nguyen Ngoc Hung—the poor soldier Hung, grown up.

We push off at eight, better than ten minutes ahead of schedule.

This brings a glow to the smile of Mr. Ming, who has been flapping around, fearful of losing someone from his precious caravan. Miss Mai gives him her perky wave of approval, and he responds with his formal two-hander and a bow worthy of a Hapsburg courtier. S. J. Perelman called the movement "Bosnian free-style."

We are heading for what we are told is Military Intelligence Headquarters to meet the slightly famous Major Nguyen Be. For ten years he was "on the road," in more discomfort than Mr. Kuralt could even dream of. Major Be's local fame comes from his ability to speak some English, which in 1965 led to his being summoned to interrogate a nineteen-year-old prisoner of war, a marine named Bobby Garwood.*

Major Be is as hard a case as you will find. He is a leathery man, fifty-three years old. He has the eyes of a point man, the graceful movements and manners of someone very careful. Not the kind of man you would want stalking you. Be is a Southerner who fought with the Viet Minh as a boy of sixteen. His family was among the few who chose to go North in 1954. He graduated from the University of Hanoi with a degree in mathematics and went back into the army in 1965. He confesses, as we head toward what was the headquarters of the 3rd Marine Division just outside of Danang, that his life did not turn out quite the way he imagined it would. "By the time

---

*Bobby Garwood was captured by Vietcong troops in September 1965. It was alleged that, during the period when American POWs were repatriated, Garwood chose to stay in Hanoi. In 1979 he said he wanted to come home, and he was allowed to return. In the United States he was arrested and charged with collaborating with the enemy, desertion, and striking a fellow POW. In 1981 Garwood was court-martialed and was convicted of the first two charges. He was fined $140,000 in back pay and dishonorably discharged. Garwood is the only POW who was tried and convicted of collaboration. He was the first marine in the history of the corps to have been convicted as a traitor.

Garwood today maintains his innocence. He admits that he knew Nguyen Be but describes him as a cruel tormentor. "If I met him on the street today, I would kill him," Garwood said from his home in California. He accuses Be of torturing him and two other prisoners, both of whom later died. He claims that Be was the right-hand man of "Mr. Ho," who was in charge of all POWs in the South. "Ho and Be were notorious among all the POWs—even the guards were frightened of them. The CIA and the Defense Intelligence Agency have files on both of them. They are considered as war criminals."

I have not been able to confirm that such files or allegations exist.

79

the war ended in 1975, I was almost forty. I had spent ten years in the jungle, here and in Laos. I married a nurse in the jungle; our son was born in the jungle. When the war was over, I knew no other life, so I stayed in the army. Now I just handle paperwork. I want to get out, but they tell me I'm too young to retire." He says he wants to go home and find out how much mathematics has changed in thirty years.

"Home to Hanoi?" I ask.

"No. Home to Saigon," says Be. The Vietnamese attachment to "home" is a bond that is hard for me to comprehend. I've always been slightly jealous of people who regard home as a place to return to, not a place to leave.

All through our drive Be refers to Saigon as Saigon, not Ho Chi Minh City. When I ask him about this, he smiles his dead-eyed smile. "Old habits," he says.

As we head up those lovely soft green hills toward the old marine headquarters, Be recalls his walk down South in 1965.

"It was terrible. We left at the worst time, at the beginning of the rainy season. On top of the thirty-kilogram [sixty-six-pound] pack, the rifle, the five grenades, and the hundred and twenty rounds of ammunition, we had to carry firewood and keep it dry. There was no other way we could cook our rice. It took two and a half months. A couple of times we were spotted by reconnaissance planes, and we were strafed by planes and, as we got farther South, by helicopters."

Be's first assignment was to a POW camp where young Bobby Garwood and another American were being held. Be was Garwood's interrogator.

"He was so young. He looked too young to be fighting. He seemed to be younger than nineteen. Bobby became my friend; we went through a lot together. We were sleeping in the same room the night he was wounded during a B-52 raid. We pulled him out and brought him to one of our hospitals."

I ask Be if it was he who convinced Garwood to join the Communist party, in fact join the Vietcong.

"I suppose I had something to do with it," says Be. "I told him the party rules, why we were fighting. But he volunteered. He was not tortured; he was not brainwashed; he volunteered to write pamphlets and to make radio broadcasts. In fact Bobby was treated better than our own officers. Our officers got half a can of rice a day; Bobby got a full can. We became very close friends. He told me all about the American holidays . . . about Christmas and Thanksgiving, about turkeys and all the special food. He cried a lot at first. He missed his family very badly. I know he has said certain things since he returned to the United States. But Bobby knows I am not a liar.

"When he was ordered to go North, he didn't want to go; he wanted to stay with us in the South. When he did go, it was really quite emotional. Bobby did what all of our people did when they went back North. He left all his best possessions. He gave me his rice pot, which was much better than mine. If you talk to him, tell him I am still alive. Give Bobby my best wishes."

The old marine base is now a boot camp for recruits of the People's Army of Vietnam. As we thread up the road, built by U.S. Navy engineers twenty-five years ago, we see squads of awkward-looking boys going through the same drills their fathers must have endured. Each carries a Soviet AK-47 assault rifle, so familiar to city boys from Beirut to East Los Angeles. Each also carries two grenades that, on close examination, turn out to be bamboo dummies. When we leave the car, they break formation, eager to find out what we are doing there. An officer explains and tells them of Major Be's war record. They crowd around, gawking in the "what the hell am I doing here" posture of all the world's draftees.

The question that occurs constantly in Vietnam is "How did these underweight farm boys frustrate the ambitions of first France and then the United States?" When American officers above the rank of captain arrived in Vietnam, they were almost universally contemptuous of the enemy. His stature was small, his equipment minimal, his manner ragged. He did not "look" like a soldier. More than one American colonel told me that "the little bastards know how to bug

81

out . . . they won't stand and fight." When these same officers left Vietnam, they had a respect that bordered on admiration for the enemy's discipline, his determination, and his courage.

After the siege of the Vietnamese special forces camp at Plei Me, Major Charles Beckwith, the chief American adviser to the garrison, told me: "I'd give anything to have two hundred VC under my command. They're the finest, most dedicated soldiers I've ever seen . . . I'd rather not comment on the performance of *my* Vietnamese forces."*

Pointing to one of the Vietcong prisoners, Beckwith told Charlie Mohr of *The New York Times*: "We ought to put this guy up on the north wall and just get rid of the government troops."

His disgust with the fighting qualities of government soldiers was central to a dilemma that was, by the end of 1965, beginning to plague the command in Saigon and the Defense Department in Washington. "Why do *their* Vietnamese fight so well, and *our* Vietnamese fight so badly?" The answer lies buried deeply in the arrogant psyche of the State Department, which in its paranoia about communism chose to defend "freedom" with monsters of its own creation. Long ago E. B. White said of such paranoia that "fear produces symptoms of the very disease we fight." The symptoms in Vietnam were the unstinting support of such gallant and inspiring leaders as Ngo Dinh Diem and Nguyen Van Thieu. Did each, even in his most profoundly selfless moment, ever utter one phrase, offer one idea that might embolden even a platoon of patriots? South Vietnam needed a Henry V. With our enthusiastic support, it chose instead a series of malevolent Baron Münchhausens. In 1962 Robert Trumbull, *The New York Times*'s old Asia hand, told David Halberstam, the paper's newest Asia hand, ". . . just remember one thing: there are no dumb Asians." A corollary to Trumbull's wisdom could well be

*Beckwith went on to become one of the most decorated soldiers in Vietnam and in 1980 was chosen to lead the raid on Tehran to free American hostages that ended in disaster.

Morley Safer

that, in foreign policy, there are no smart Americans. Or very few and they are usually placed under suspicion. What is it in the American soul that finds corrupt fanatics so captivating—Batista, Noriega, Mobutu. How did we ever neglect the Ayatollah Khomeini?

Major Be has brought with him a large military map of the area around Danang. From 1968 until the end of the war he practiced his craft in these mountains. He was the adviser to a Vietcong company commander whose job was to ambush American and South Vietnamese patrols. He spreads the map on the shoulder of the road and squats down in that knee-wrenching position the Vietnamese can hold for hours without showing discomfort.

I ask Be about ambushes, were they small, hit-and-run operations?

"No . . . always in an ambush you must have a greater force. If you ambush a company you must have at least a company and a half. You must have good intelligence, first of all, so that you lay the claymore mines where they will do the most damage. The purpose of the ambush was to kill the enemy, of course, but the most important thing for us was documents, to get maps and documents."

I ask Be if he ever went into Danang during the war.

"Yes, because I speak English I went into Danang seven times with the intelligence officer. I also walked onto the marine air base twice to make maps. It was important to know what changes the Americans were making on the base."

Be is so specific with numbers . . . seven times into Danang, twice to the air base . . . he had told me he'd been in five ambushes. I wonder about this and then it becomes quite obvious. When you are scared shitless, detail becomes engraved in the memory.

Be, unlike other veterans I've met, seems utterly cold-blooded when he talks about the war. He says he doesn't know if he killed any Americans, as it was generally at night when he was engaged in this sport.

"There were plenty of dead when we went to retrieve documents and weapons, but I don't know if I killed any," he says. Then, almost

83

as if to reassure me that he had no qualms about this activity, he says: "But I must tell you, I welcomed the chance to kill Americans."

I am surprised when we get up to leave that Be tells me that he dreams about the war every night. I had mentioned that some Americans are having a rough time of it. That some men are haunted by nightmares, others feel abandoned, rejected, hostile to the country that sent them to war.

"Some of our veterans have such feelings," he says, "but I do not . . . but I have this dream all the time, two dreams. I dream of the five ambushes. And I always see the same thing. I see my men lying dead on the path.

"The other dream is of an American air strike in the mountains, and I see my son badly wounded by the bombing. It is the same dream over and over again. Such a thing did not happen to my son, but when I go to sleep my mind invents it."

This is told without passion. It is almost as if he is delivering an intelligence report to a senior officer. There is no imagery or embellishment . . . and above all, he has no regrets. His eyes have what American GIs called "the thousand-yard stare." It is said to be what happens after experiencing a certain amount of killing. I think Nguyen Be was born with it. With a few hundred battalion commanders like him leading "our" Vietnamese, the outcome of the war might have been different.

12

"You Just Shat on the Flag"

En route Danang, 11:00 A.M.: Why am I keeping these notes? So much has been agonized over, apologized for, condemned, and lied about. The only truth in war, I decide, is the one offered by Senator Hiram Johnson in 1917: "The first casualty in war is truth."

It seems to me that as much has been written about how the war was covered as how it was fought. It has been proposed that television in Vietnam changed forever the way wars will be conducted and the way they will be perceived. I am not so sure about all that. In Vietnam, television, most of journalism, merely confirmed to Americans that the entire affair had a certain stench to it. Westmoreland and many others fully believed the stench came from the lies, inexperience, and manipulations of journalists. Dean Rusk, the former secretary of state, said that reporters must decide whose side they were on.

Robert Elegant, a former reporter and now the author of fat

novels, wrote a vicious piece in *Encounter* in 1981 blaming the loss of the war on reporters whose mission was to discredit the United States. I responded with a commentary, perhaps just a touch intemperate, that Mr. Elegant's article would appeal to the few remaining admirers of Dr. Joseph Goebbels.

In general, those who aim to kill the messengers shoot themselves in the feet. But more and more revisionism is at work, and the truth, if not dead, is at the very least missing in action.

During the drive back to Danang, Major Be tells me that he has never talked to a journalist before "except for fraternal Socialist journalists after the war." I smile at this and Be laughs. Miss Mai stares straight ahead, not sure what this means, this unspoken dialogue. I am not entirely certain myself, but I imagine windy gentlemen from Tass and Tanjug, the Yugoslav news agency, sending puffed-up memoirs and dispatches from an imaginary front. During the war there were all kinds of rumors of Soviet correspondents and cameramen—even advisers—being seen with Vietcong units, but nothing was ever confirmed. The only person I can recall who regularly filed from Hanoi was Wilfred Burchett, a big bumbling Australian Communist. American officials discounted everything Wilf wrote as being filtered through a Marxist maze. Little did they know that it was gin that was his constant companion, mentor, and political editor. For all of his goofy ideas about the world, he had an Aussie's gift for laughter, for keeping a bar open after hours, and for never picking up the tab. He was a fixture in the bar at the Hotel Lutetia in Paris during the peace talks in 1968, and occasionally quite a good source. It has been said that Henry Kissinger used him as a means of making contact with Hanoi.

When Major Be left us I asked Miss Mai to ask the driver to take us to the Danang press center. This was an establishment set up by the Marine Corps at the beginning of 1965 to accommodate journalists working in I Corps, the marine area of responsibility.

The place squatted on the riverbank, protected from God-knows-

Morley Safer

what by double coils of rusting concertina wire. There were two rows of dilapidated motel rooms, perhaps twenty in all, separated by a central campus that was a quagmire twelve months of the year. At the far end, the river side, was a dining room and a bar with a broken jukebox. The three networks and the American wire services kept permanent rooms at the press center. Our landlord was the U.S. Marine Corps, represented by a major and a gunnery sergeant. The marines in turn rented the place from a Frenchman who, until the day it became a press center, had operated a brothel there. He was an opium-emaciated man in his fifties who kept one room for himself and a favorite sixteen-year-old Vietnamese girl. The couple left after only a few weeks. The last I saw of him was an evening in March 1965. He was packing his car, a well-dented Citroën Deux-Chevaux.

"Why are you leaving?" I asked.

"This used to be a respectable house," he said, "very clean, but look at it now . . . the animals have taken it over. The rent is very good; I have no complaints about that, but I hate to see my life's work destroyed. I will go to Saigon, where perhaps I can begin again. A good whorehouse is hard to find these days."

The press center recalls few good memories. Beyond the war being fought and reported outside the concertina wire, there were continuing skirmishes, ambushes, and psychological warfare being waged inside.

By the mid-sixties reporters were regarded by the military, at best, as prima donnas out to make reputations for themselves or, at worst, as a kind of Vietcong fifth column bent on demoralizing the American public. The reporters regarded the marines who ran the press center and the officers who hung out there as barroom heroes who talked a much better war than they fought. In the field, I think, there was a mutual respect between correspondents and combat marines. The feelings required no verbal communication. At the press center there was nothing *but* conversation. It was fueled by cheap liquor and high-stakes poker. The broken jukebox got that way one night when a marine major emptied his .45 automatic into its delicate electronic soul.

My difficulties with the management of the press center were sparked by a report I filed in August 1965, on the burning of the hamlet of Cam Ne by the marines. That broadcast on the *CBS Evening News* ignited a powder keg of suspicion, even hatred, that continues to this day.

The only time in Vietnam that I carried a weapon was on my visit back to Danang following the broadcast of the Cam Ne incident. I had been told there might be "a little accident." I lay awake in my bunk all night with a loaded 9 mm FN automatic pistol on the night table, scared stiff that I would plug some friendly drunk who might come to call . . . or worse, shoot myself trying to release the safety.

The Cam Ne story was broadcast over and over again in the United States and overseas. It was seized upon by Hanoi as a propaganda tool and by scoundrels of the left and right, in the Pentagon and on campuses. To the peace movement it was The Revealed Truth of the administration's spiraling fall to fascism. To the war movement it was blatant evidence of the perfidy of journalism. Lyndon Johnson accused Dr. Frank Stanton, the president of CBS, of having "shat on the American flag."

It all started so innocently. Innocently. That word applied to Vietnam gives me the chills. An August dawn, rousting myself and Ha Thuc Can and the sound man, a boy named Thien, from our room at the press center. Milky coffee, French bread dipped into it, and a short ride in the barely mobile CBS jeep to a staging area along a creek a few miles south of the airport. The marines are assembling in amtracks, amphibious armored personnel carriers.

This will hardly be a surprise attack. The marines are joking, smoking; one man is playing music on a tape recorder fixed to his helmet. The Walkman has not yet been invented for the private entertainment of the stealthy. No matter, for the clanking and groaning of the amtracks give a good mile's warning that the Yanks are coming.

Morley Safer

Standing in the well of the amtrack I ask a lieutenant about our mission.

"We are going to Cam Ne," he says. "Search and destroy. Especially destroy. We've been taking fire from there every time we go by, and the gook head honcho in these parts told us to go teach them a lesson." The word "gook" in the early days was used to describe only the Vietcong; it very quickly came to include all Vietnamese, including the head of government.

He shows me Cam Ne on his large-scale map. It is not a single village but a collection of hamlets, with each cluster of black squares on the map representing a separate small community. The map designated them as Cam Ne 1, 2, 3, and 4.

"Which Cam Ne?" I ask.

"All of them."

The amtracks spread out, slithering through flooded paddies, sliding down irrigation canals. We are not going to surround the hamlets, but approach them from three sides.

The ramp goes down, and Can and Thien and I, tethered together by microphone, power supply, and sound synchronization cables, follow the first wave of marines onto a patch of dry ground. About a hundred and fifty yards away, behind a tree line, we see smoke rising from cooking fires and the roofs of a collection of huts—"hootches" is the unofficial military jargon. The first wave approaches, spread out in a long single green line; the second wave is perhaps fifty yards behind.

We hear a few distant "bap-baps," the unmistakable signature of automatic weapons. Then from all around, the echoes doubling the effect, there is an enormous "whoosh!" of fire and the deeper thumps of outgoing mortar rounds and rockets. To my immediate right a marine is down . . . farther down the line two more have been hit. A sergeant runs down the line shouting then screaming to cease fire. The closest wounded marine is writhing in pain, still conscious. He's been shot in the buttocks; farther down I see medics treating the two

89

others, one wounded in the buttocks, the other in the back. There can be little doubt that we have been hit by so-called friendly fire.

We walk into Cam Ne. Mud alleys separate the huts. A black-toothed old woman runs, surprisingly gracefully, toward me, tears streaming down her face, hands outstretched, pleading. The marines are rousting people out of the huts with their rifles, some with bayonets fixed. The houses are all the same: woven reeds plastered with mud and roofed with thatch. There is one cement-block building with a tin roof. It looks like a schoolhouse. There are other cement structures that appear to be long-abandoned foundations for houses. As people stumble out of houses, marines, some with flame-throwers, others using matches, yet others with Zippo lighters, begin systematically to set fire to each hut. The villagers are in shock. A few run to flaming houses to rescue valuables, a plastic bag of rice, a dog that had been tied to a post. Not a pet, an evening meal. But mostly the people just stare. An amtrack approaches a mud lane. It cannot get in between the trees so it detours around, looking for an opening on some high ground, and heads for it, grinding up a small graveyard. Headstones lie scattered. Can and Thien and I, still tethered together, walk down an alley against the flow of villagers, some with hands raised in the air, being prodded along by marines. About ten yards in front of the last house in the clearing, four marines are crouched in a drainage ditch, three of them with rifles aimed at the house. The fourth, in these cramped quarters, has unstrapped his flamethrower and is fiddling with the switches. A lieutenant comes running up—crouched, and flops into the ditch.

"What's happening?" he asks.

"We heard voices from that hootch," a private says.

The lieutenant empties a magazine from his automatic rifle into the house, and bits of dried mud and thatch go flying.

Now the voices are very clear, but not like human voices at all. A wailing sound, high and clear, followed by a chorus of keening and the rattling sound of a baby crying, but it is almost an animal sound.

90

"Torch it," the lieutenant says. The private with the flamethrower rises from the ditch, thick gloves holding the nozzle waist high. The three of us cannot believe what is about to happen. Ha Thuc Can sets his Auricon camera down on the path.

"Wait," he says to the lieutenant. "Please wait." Standing in front of the ditch, in front of the flamethrower, he cups his hands and shouts in Vietnamese: "Come out, come out now, and you will be safe. If you stay inside you will be killed."

This only makes the wailing inside increase.

"Get out of the way," the lieutenant says.

Can walks to the door of the hut, lies down on the ground, and begins to talk softly to the empty doorway.

"Please, come out now . . . they will not hurt you if you come out now."

Now there is silence. The marines, emboldened by Can's almost casual stroll to the doorway, leave their cover and join us, standing, rifles aimed at the doorway. In the half-darkness inside are some shattered cooking pots, two or three cots, and a hammock slung against a side wall. The cooking fire is smoldering, whatever was in the pots has doused most of the fire. Next to the fire a crack begins to widen in the dirt floor. As the trapdoor rises, ancient eyes appear, then a nose, mouth, and wispy beard. A marine switches on a flash-light, and an old man steps out onto the dirt floor, hands clasped over his head, then two children, then a young woman holding a baby. The baby is crying. The mother is holding a filthy bloody cloth to its side.

The lieutenant orders the family to get out, to join the others on the main path. They stare at him . . . now all of them have placed their hands over their heads.

Can retrieves his camera, and we three are wired together again. The marines move back about twenty feet with us. The flamethrower belches like some eager dragon, and the house is consumed.

That evening I shipped the film report and narration of the Cam

91

Ne story to New York and telexed the story in written form. The reaction to it was incendiary. The Defense Department laid siege to Fred Friendly, then president of CBS News, demanding that I be recalled from Vietnam. The marines felt they'd been stabbed in the back.

Their afteraction report and my television broadcast described two totally different operations. The marines claimed that the only huts that were burned were fortified Vietcong bunkers from which the marines received fire. Others, said the report, were damaged by accident in the course of heated battle. The report also maintained that all civilians were removed before any houses were destroyed. The report did not include the fact that what pitiful fortifications did exist in Cam Ne—mainly those cement foundations—had been paid for with American aid. The marines were not aware that Cam Ne was part of the fortified hamlet program that the United States had urged the Diem government to undertake. The marines, at least the troops sent into Cam Ne, were also unaware, as was I, that the operation had been requested by the province chief, who wanted the hamlet punished for nonpayment of taxes. This was discovered months later by Richard Critchfield, who then worked for the *Washington Star.* The marines and I agreed only on the facts that there was a single fatality, a ten-year-old boy, and that there were five Vietnamese wounded and four prisoners taken.

We also agreed on the fact that no one who could possibly be described as a soldier had been captured, dead or alive, and not a single weapon or even an empty cartridge case had been found—not even inside the so-called bunkers and firing positions that had been "cleaned out." The marine report neglected to say that the four prisoners taken were men in their late sixties or early seventies and that all five wounded were women, plump housewives, not daring little teenage sappers. I had reported one hundred fifty houses destroyed. The marines claimed only thirty. Charlie Mohr of *The New York Times* flew over the hamlet the following day and reported three hundred houses destroyed.

The marines were quick to retaliate. First with direct threats at the press center. A drunken major stood outside our room a few nights later screaming "Communist Broadcasting System" as he emptied his pistol in the air. Had the place not been filled with other reporters, I genuinely believe that Ha Thuc Can and I would have been killed.

Then Marine Corps headquarters in Washington claimed that the film of a marine setting fire to a roof with a Zippo lighter had been faked: that I had given the marine the lighter and had asked him to burn down the house. This was quickly squelched when the private in question could not be produced to repeat the story. It was comforting to know that *Semper Fidelis* still applied in the Corps, at least among the "other ranks."

Despite the furor, two days after the operation, the marines allowed me to interview some of the men who had taken part in it. I asked: "Do you have any private doubts, any regrets about some of these people you are leaving homeless?"

A marine answered: "You can't have feelings of remorse for these people. They are an enemy until proven innocent . . . I feel no remorse. I don't imagine anybody else does. You can't do your job and feel pity for these people."

When that report was broadcast, the marines responded that the man I talked to had been lured into an indiscreet answer by a misleading question.

Gordon Manning, who was then a vice president at CBS, demonstrated great resolve during that period. In a craft that has come to be dominated by cost-conscious sycophants, Manning stands out as an executive whose first priority is the story. At the time of Cam Ne, when executive sinew at CBS was in danger of turning to treacle, he reminded one and all in New York, and me in Saigon, of Harry Truman's remark that "as an effective public relations arm, the Marine Corps is second only to Stalin."

Manning's effectiveness is such that he does not make a good "corporate fit," so he was fired from CBS in 1974 and went on to greater glory at NBC. He got Gorbachev to sit down with Tom Brokaw, providing the general secretary would not have to receive any more telegrams from Comrade Manning. The Manning telegrams have become legendary as Manningrams throughout American journalism and both the Russian and Chinese Politburos.

The most outraged reaction to Cam Ne came from the White House. The morning after the broadcast the president of the United States, Lyndon Johnson, telephoned his good friend and member of the president's Advisory Commission on the United States Information Agency, Frank Stanton, who was also the president of CBS.

"Hello, Frank, this is your president."

"Yes, Mr. President."

"Frank, you trying to fuck me?" The president then went on to give Stanton, one of the coolest, most aloof men I have ever known, a dreadful tongue lashing. He described graphically how CBS and I, and by inference Stanton himself, had publicly desecrated the flag. A few days later he summoned Stanton to the White House and in a small office off the Oval Office, with Bill Moyers, then his press secretary, continued the harangue. The meeting then took a much darker turn. Johnson threatened that, unless CBS got rid of me and "cleaned up its act," the White House would "go public" with information about Safer's "Communist ties."

Johnson claimed that he and Moyers "had the goods" on me as a result of an investigation launched by the FBI, the CIA, and the Royal Canadian Mounted Police.

In fact there was an investigation that produced nothing, except perhaps the fact that politically the Safers were an extremely conservative bunch. Johnson, with Moyers's help, was simply bluffing.

The affair put Stanton in an extremely difficult position. He was a friend and adviser to the president and was perfectly aware of the vindictive nature of the man; at the same time he was a staunch protector of the newsroom. To Stanton's and Fred Friendly's credit, none of the heat that was put on them was felt by me half a world away. I was oblivious to the impact of the Cam Ne story until months later, when I returned to New York for a rest and was stunned that people were still talking about it.

Bill Moyers's role in the affair has since made me feel slightly uneasy in his presence. On two occasions I asked him about it, and each time he laughed it off as just a fit of temper by the president and that he, Moyers, was the good guy trying to play peacemaker.

Not quite true. After the Cam Ne story, Murray Fromson, then a CBS News correspondent, was asked by New York to drop in on Moyers in Washington and to try to smooth the troubled relationship between CBS News and the White House. Fromson had become friendly with Moyers during the 1960 election campaign. The meeting had hardly begun when Moyers snapped at Fromson: "Why do you have to use foreigners to cover that war? A Canadian and a Vietnamese?"

Such a remark can be dismissed as a bit of good soldiering by a servant loyal to the president in the candid heat of the moment.

After all, in 1965 Moyers was a politician whose agenda would not preclude dealing in a certain amount of disinformation. He may or may not have been responsible for the manner in which the Cam Ne story continued to produce aftershocks.

In the early 1980s a team of researchers working on a book about coverage of the war went to visit Graham Martin, the last American ambassador to South Vietnam. In the course of their questions, Martin, on whom I have never laid eyes, told them:

"Different reporters had different motivations, of course. The question of Morley Safer is interesting. I knew him well. I also knew he was a KGB agent—so did the White House . . . but all that is of course totally irrelevant."

The story was never used. Martin was in poor health, an eccentric and bitter man. But a few years later much the same thing was said by Dean Rusk, secretary of state during the Johnson years.

To this day Rusk believes the entire Cam Ne story was staged. He

95

says that I convinced a Marine Corps unit to bring in some Vietnamese refugees to an abandoned village that the marines used for training exercises, that I then asked the marines to torch the village, and that, being susceptible, well-meaning young Americans, they obliged.

Rusk maintains that it was "common knowledge at the White House that the reporter was a questionable character with ties to the Soviet intelligence apparatus. . . . The White House had its own intelligence on him but for reasons I can't recall, they never used it."

I find it hard to believe that Bill Moyers would engage in character assassination over one brief evening news broadcast—even given the political imperatives of the moment. But I confess, I find it harder not to believe it. His part in Lyndon Johnson and J. Edgar Hoover's bugging of Martin Luther King's private life, the leaks to the press and diplomatic corps, the surveillance of civil rights groups at the 1964 Democratic convention, and his request for damaging information from Hoover on members of the Goldwater campaign suggest that he was not only a good soldier but a gleeful retainer feeding the appetites of Lyndon Johnson. It's all too confusing. Bill Moyers, the sometimes overly pious public defender of liberal virtue, the First Amendment, and the rights of minorities, playing the role of Iago.

Cam Ne continues to linger. To this day, Fred Friendly, professor emeritus at Columbia University, former president of CBS News, uses the Cam Ne story as a teaching device. Weeks after the broadcast, in his typically overzealous way, he described Vietnam as "Morley Safer's war."

It's interesting. One story that I came upon in the most routine way, a story offered up by the marines themselves, became, to some people anyway, symbolic not only of the war but also of the coming of age of television. Proof that the road to glory or damnation may often be paved with no intentions at all.

These are the pitifully vain reflections of a not-quite-grown-up but nevertheless aging reporter as he stares at the press center, at this old

96

battleground of the spirit through its new wrought-iron gates. I cannot see a trace of the old structure. It is gone, replaced by a fish-processing plant, the manager of which tells me that it is forbidden to enter without a letter of permission from the Ministry of Health. Brothel, press center, dead fish.

13

Devi in Blue Jeans

Danang, 12:30 P.M.: The Cham Museum faces the press center. It has survived better than I expected. It holds some wonderful treasures—mainly stone carvings—that I feared would have been taken as booty by retreating Vietnamese, advancing Vietnamese, avaricious correspondents, or, that most unscrupulous breed of all, The Dealers in Antiquities. The Hong Kong and Bangkok subculture is exceeded in ruthlessness only by its cousins in Athens and Rome. Men of scholarship all, they will not give a second thought to grave robbery, document forgery, or grievously harming those who get in their way. Their specialty is vanished or vanishing cultures. The Etruscans are fair game as are the Navajos and, on the coastal plain of Vietnam, the temples of the Cham people, the relics of the Champa Empire. I know a man, a dealer, who in the early seventies hired a company of Vietnamese infantry supported by armor to provide security for a foray deep into Vietcong territory in Binh Dinh Province. His mission was to pillage a Cham temple. He accomplished his task without

98

incident. I was not there, but in my imagination I see a train of armored personnel carriers lurching through jungle and rice paddy, laden high with frescoes chiseled from walls and goddesses hammered from their plinths. It is witnessing a gang rape of history.

The poor old Cham, so little is known of them. What is can be seen in the airy halls of the museum in Danang. Drifting through, it is easy to understand why these treasures survived . . . they were too massive, too heavy for even an armored personnel carrier, though here and there a head has been chopped off. The place remains a cool escape. Occasionally in the sixties I came in with a beer and a baguette stuffed with cheese and tomatoes for a private withdrawal from the war. Quite soothing really, surrounded by these smooth, rounded women, each striking a pose more erotic than the last one, like some porno contest from the past. Near each of these women trying so hard to please stands an erect lingam at stony attention. There is plenty beyond the erotica . . . soldier-kings and enormous frescoes of battle scenes depicting Cham horsemen and archers doing away with various Chinese, Vietnamese, and Khmer. Wishful wartime propaganda of the tenth century. The Cham were as fierce as they were artistic and libidinous, and everyone seemed to hate them. The Cochin Chinese pushed them south to Binh Dinh, then the Vietnamese took over for a little internal family slaughter, followed by Khmer from the west . . . who always preferred wounded prey. Then came Kublai Khan from the sea. With him, it wasn't personal; he simply ravaged the entire coast and anyone who got in his way. The Vietnamese, having been diverted by a brief dust-up with the Chinese, then moved in to mop up, and by the end of the fifteenth century the Cham were finished, extinguished as a nation.

But of course, not quite. Henri Mouhot, among the bravest and most obsessed of nineteenth-century explorers, had the rather madcap idea that the Cham were one of the lost tribes of Israel. The Jews, like the Cham, just cannot be left alone. I once knew an Irishman

99

who made the same claim about the origins of his Celtic forbears.

Mouhot, tramping through the untracked margins of Cambodia and Vietnam in search of new insects and herbs for his patron, the Royal Geographic Society in London, had a private agenda. In July 1861, as he paused to rest at a French Catholic mission station on the Vietnamese side of what is now the Cambodian border, he noted in his diary:

> As for the [Cham], I made endeavors to investigate their origin, and also the traces which I supposed to exist in Cambodia of Israelite migrations. Monsignor Miche (who'd suffered terribly in his attempts to convert the Vietnamese) told me that he had never met any Jews in the country, but that he had found in one of the sacred books of the Cambodians, the judgment of Solomon exactly recorded and attributed to one of their kings who had become a god, after having been, according to their ideas of metempsychosis, an ape and an elephant. What is the origin of these strange people? Whence came they?

Mouhot goes on to relate that he discovers a copy of *The Life of Abbé Gagelin*, another of those martyrs who gave his life, bit by painful bit, trying to convert the Cochin Chinese to Catholicism. The abbé claimed to have found the descendants of the Cham . . . for Mouhot it was confirmation of a pet theory:

> I found what I had long been in search of and I extract the following passages from Abbé Gagelin's letters: "It is difficult for strangers to observe the domestic life of these people; but it is said they practice circumcision, observe the Sabbath and abstain from the flesh of pork. It is even said they possess the Pentateuch, but this I dare not affirm. Are they an ancient colony of Ishmaelites or Idumeans? Are they an offshoot of Israelites thrown on these shores? These questions are worthy of consideration. However it may be, their care to preserve their traditions pure from all alloy, and their obstinate persistence in error, render them worthy of a Jewish origin."

100

I wonder if the Arab apologists in the State Department are onto this little gem.

Will we see a learned paper from some fledgling George Ball blaming the loss of Vietnam on Israeli intransigence, a millennium or so removed? Will they reach back to the dusty bones of Abbé Gagelin to prove how patient and understanding is their friend, the murderous Mr. Arafat?

The fixed ecstatic smiles of the prancing, squatting, and aerobically inventive Cham maidens and the equally joyful faces of the archers beam down on these meager observations. Miss Mai meantime has climbed up on a plinth that held one of the larger goddesses whose head has been neatly sawed off. She tucks in behind the ample lady and places her own head on the goddess's neck. Our still cameras snap away at this new goddess of minders, whose ministry pass has the magical power to reduce elephantine civil servants to chattering obsequious monkeys.

Our entire caravan takes turns striking this pose, but none does it with quite the effect of Miss Mai. She is the goddess Devi, mother of Shiva—the most benevolent and ferocious of women. Her head has been reconnected here in Danang—Devi in blue jeans.

Flashbacks

14

"Surely the Gods Live Here"

Marble Mountain, 2:00 P.M.: Marble Mountain—or more accurately, the Marble Mountains of Danang, look strangely out of place. They are most likely the last few gasps of an eruption stretching down from Kwangsi Province in China. Chinese is what these mountains are, bearing no resemblance to anything in North America or Europe, or even to the mountains of Japan. These look to be the creations of a great Chinese master of ink and brush. Wild swirls of soaring pinnacles and rounded, almost animal-head shapes. They seem to grow out of nothing. There is no gradual rise in terrain, only blobs, thousands of them stuck on the landscape.

In an old notebook I find some lines I scribbled more than twenty years ago: "It's as if the gods, carrying these absurd heaps of molten rock from their equatorial melting place to their allotted destination, had dropped a few of them unnoticed on the way." I have no idea where this comes from. The lines are in quotes—but not a clue as to who is the author.

102

On a small plain on the leeward side of the mountains the Marine Corps operated the busiest helicopter pad in Vietnam. Not a trace of all that activity remains except for the tarmac, which has become a crazy-paving of cracks. The Marble Mountain helipad, like so many American landmarks in Vietnam, bears not even the suggestion that so many served, so many died, so much blood and hope were spent. Day and night the dust swirled around this broken concrete . . . ammunition and great plastic bladders of water going out, body bags and wounded coming in. The wind was constant from the whipping rotors. You could be guaranteed a one-way trip to anywhere in I Corps from Marble Mountain. The return trip was, as the airlines say, space available. Wounded had first priority. There was usually space on the so-called meat wagons, the aircraft carrying body bags. I took such a trip once—out of necessity—and vowed never again to book such awful passage.

Now, gazing across the cracking pavement with its backdrop of fantasy mountains, the place has a postnuclear look to it. I imagine that if the day-after ever happens this is what the world will be. Parking lots and mountains of marble will survive. This journey so far has been surprisingly elating. The absence of bitterness and the absence of danger and noise and stink of war are partly the reason. But today, under low clouds with a sea mist rolling in, bad memories fill the mind.

The marines, the poor abused marines. They arrived in force in early 1965, on the beach about a mile from here. "Splashed ashore" is the favored wire service phrase that is meant to conjure up the bloody and heroic island assaults of the Second World War. When they landed here, there were no enemy snipers or mine fields. Only cameramen and reporters fetched up from Saigon to record the event. I think it was the first time I heard the words "photo opportunity." The command in Saigon felt that the sight of marines "splashing ashore" would be a familiar reassuring one for folks back home. For Marine Corps recruiters it would be an especially stirring device

103

to remind eighteen-year-olds that they, too, could stand in the same salty Pacific that John Wayne had liberated so many times before.

The marines were well disciplined but were not in very good condition. On the trek up to their positions that first day, they took serious casualties from the heat. Mercifully, they did not have to fight their way into Vietnam. They were also utterly untrained for the assignment. No one seemed to tell them there were "friendlies" around. The decision to put an elite assault force into static positions in a highly populated area is up there in military blundering with the disastrous Beirut expedition, years later.

Despite moments of rancor, marines have always had my admiration. In Vietnam they were given the worst assignments and the most outdated equipment. South Vietnamese popular forces had the new M-16 rifles before the marines got them. The new lightweight combat boots were more easily obtainable in the Saigon black market than they were in a Marine Corps depot. They were the least educated, best disciplined troops, and they fought bravely, despite the ambiguity of their mission and the weakness of their leadership at the highest levels of command. Their commandant, General Wallace Greene, was blindly optimistic and badly advised. Marine Corps General Victor Krulak was the special assistant for counterinsurgency to the Joint Chiefs of Staff and later became the commander of the Pacific fleet force. He was a small man who tended to strut—an absolute hound for publicity. He seemed oblivious to both the military and the political realities of the terrain on which he was supposed to be the expert and to which he and others committed the marines.

Krulak was sent to Vietnam by President Kennedy in 1963 to assess the capabilities of Diem's forces; he reported back that the situation was well in hand.

Barely two months later Diem was overthrown, and there was the very real danger that the Vietcong would seize the northern half of South Vietnam.

Many years later, I was flying from Parris Island, South Carolina,

104

back to Washington with General Al Gray, the Marine Corps commandant. General Gray is the first commandant to have risen through the ranks. He is a shy man, suspicious of publicity, well read on the arts of war, and, he says, determined not to let "his" marines be frittered away on dubious expeditions. I had reminded him of a number of recent episodes that could come under the heading of "dubious." Vietnam, the Desert One fiasco—the failed attempt to rescue the hostages held in Iran—the questionable victory of American arms over the ragtag garrison in Grenada, and the slaughter of marines at Beirut Airport.

"What would you do if the president or the Joint Chiefs wanted to order your marines into a situation you thought was wrong for them? Would you go along?"

"No. I would quit first."

I was not sure he meant it. But he has so much affection for the men under his command and so much contempt for the kind of officer who went along with bad strategic decisions to serve worse political ones, that he just might. General Gray is reluctant to comment on the actions of his predecessors—the bond, the loyalty to the Corps is almost mystical in its power. But he quietly fumes over the debacles. The men sent to Beirut were his men; he had commanded them just before they were shipped out. He turned scarlet just thinking about it.

Al Gray served with distinction for three years in Vietnam, trying to make the best of a dreadful predicament. He arrived in early 1965, a businesslike commander of an artillery battalion. The Corps sent him back in 1975, just before the collapse, to supervise the evacuation of the American embassy in Saigon. It was not the Vietcong, but Al Gray, who laid the explosive charges that blew to hell what was left of value in America's bumbling interlude in Southeast Asia.

When the marines arrived at Marble Mountain in 1965, few officers had the restraint of Al Gray. They were full of phony bravado. Lots of talk about kicking ass and killing gooks. They had been

105

conditioned to have an open and easy relationship with reporters and a hunger for publicity, not so much for their men, it seemed, as for themselves. Instead of drinking buddies and cheerleaders, they faced a slightly hostile, often pompous, but nevertheless serious group of experienced journalists who questioned everything, most of all the presence of the Marine Corps.

Almost every officer I met in those first months grandstanded in one way or another to get profiled in newspapers or featured on evening news broadcasts. It was as if their entire course of familiarization on Vietnam had been given by screening Second World War movies. Even the chaplains worked overtime mugging for the camera. I saw one in neatly pressed fatigues reach down and cover his uniform and face with mud as he saw a camera crew approaching. The same man then placed a sign on his tent: "Your ass may belong to the USMC, but your soul belongs to God. Please walk in." This had the desired effect, not of creating a stream of born-again leathernecks, but of getting the good padre's picture taken by the dozen or so photo-opportunistic cameramen. The right buttons can so easily be pressed.

The disillusion came soon enough, and it crushed the long-held belief that American reporters and American servicemen were brothers in arms in an unquestioned crusade. That relationship was yet another sacred icon that sank into the mud of Vietnam. Marines expected a Rudyard Kipling or at the very least an Ernie Pyle to record and embellish their expedition. They got an R. W. Apple, Jr., of *The New York Times*, Jack Foisie of the *Los Angeles Times*, and Peter Arnett of the Associated Press. The Corps felt confused then betrayed when it realized that marines were being covered not as brave participants in a great patriotic war but as less than perfect pawns in a dreadful misadventure. There were exceptions like Keyes Beech, then of the *Chicago Daily News*, who considered it his duty, I suppose, to report the war as favorably as possible. I cannot say this was reflected in every piece of copy he sent back—we rarely saw the results of each other's work—but he would engage in long and well-oiled tirades against the "Communist tendencies" of his younger colleagues. Keyes also sported a Marine Corps fatigue cap that, if it did not contain actual sand from Iwo Jima, was at the very least kept as weather-beaten as possible. He wore such paraphernalia with great pride and would not brook even the most harmless ribbing over his getup. Keyes was rewarded for his efforts and included in a not-so-secret Military Assistance Command list of "reliable" correspondents.

Not all the reporting challenged the war and the effort. Even the most skeptical correspondents did their share of upbeat reports, stories of the genuine valor, humanity, and comradeship that were the rule among most of the men who served in Vietnam. New York editors, particularly television editors, had an enormous appetite for combat stories and for both heart-wrenching and amusing "soft" stories.

Not a mile from where I am standing at the Marble Mountain helipad, I recall Roger Staubach, the 1963 Heisman Memorial Trophy winner and future legend of the Dallas Cowboys, being trotted out in response to at least a dozen correspondents' requests for a moment of his time. Staubach, an Annapolis graduate, served his tour as a navy supply corps lieutenant in Danang and Chu Lai. The poor man was compelled to throw footballs for at least a score of cameramen while marine and navy information officers and mud-splattered grunts looked on. It must have been embarrassing, even humiliating, for Staubach, tossing long perfect spirals to amateur wide receivers who'd been pressed into service for the occasion. The performance was accompanied by the continuous approval of a battery of outgoing artillery.

It was the perfect television feature. Here was Young America, the epitome of achievement, serving his country, but finding time to keep his arm in a state of readiness for its future efforts with "America's Team."

There was small appetite—at least among the networks—for the

107

political story from Vietnam. It took too long to tell and involved characters who spoke no English and belonged to parties, factions, faiths, and sects that to New York seemed irrelevant to the continuing story of the American war. The war, after all, was a domestic story . . . it was only incidental that it was being fought so far away. The Vietnamese were, both by military design and by editorial imperative, mere bystanders. The local political story was received by New York with tedium and broadcast reluctantly.

That attitude was understandable. The government itself was a loose coalition of six parties ranging from the Ethnic Minority Solidarity Movement to the Vietnam Humanist Social Revolutionary party. Nine parties were in the approved opposition, plus more that were, for various reasons, outlawed. It was a nightmare to report, but the fact that it was so rarely reported, except by people with the space and patience of a Bob Shaplen of *The New Yorker*, made for a significant gap in the public's knowledge of the place, a place it was being asked to sacrifice so much for. The Congress and the Defense Department were equally oblivious to the Byzantium that South Vietnam had become.

War was the thing, for editors and for everyone else. The so-called bang-bang story in either victory or defeat—it did not matter which—got the blood up. When congressmen came to Vietnam the last thing they wanted was to spend time with plodding Vietnamese deputies. In fact being photographed with this or that particular politician might later prove to be a liability. It was important, however, to be seen with Westmoreland and the troops. In a sense the Vietnamese were invisible.

This ghost of an airfield, so silent now, was on the "must see" list for important visitors to Vietnam. Editors on ten-day junkets were taken here; invited guests of the Pentagon like Joe Alsop, the most reliably hawkish of the Washington columnists, were accorded all the honors of a two-star general. If there had been a *Michelin Guide to Vietnam*, Marble Mountain would definitely have had three stars and been marked as *Vaut le voyage*. It was a vivid demonstration of taxpayers' dollars and sons at work. Novelist John Steinbeck, thought by the State Department to be favorably disposed to the war, was escorted to each of the four tactical war zones, allowed to fire all the weapons and play with all the toys, and was then expected to return to California and spread the gospel of America's selfless mission in Southeast Asia.

Much the same treatment, but with even greater intensity, was given to Walter Cronkite on his first visit in 1965. The ancient military practice of dulling the brains of visitors with endless briefings, using opaque military jargon and strings of incomprehensible map coordinates, supported by sports metaphors and locker-room optimism, did not succeed in making him a believer. He was too skeptical, too savvy, and had too sensitive a shit-detector to be taken in. Cronkite has the gift of asking aggressive questions without ever seeming to be aggressive. But Walter can be diverted by machinery, by things with wheels and wings, and especially by things that float, and the military saw to it that he had a chance to see and use everything, go on air strikes, be made to feel an "insider."

His itinerary was designed to keep him away as much as possible from correspondents and others permanently based in Vietnam who were considered to be naysayers. It did not entirely work. I managed to arrange at least two meetings to counter the lies and bogus optimism that had been so carefully orchestrated for him. One was with an Army officer based in the Iron Triangle for two years who slipped into Saigon clandestinely and met with us in the Continental Palace Hotel. In terse but emotional language he catalogued the disaster to come. "With a million men here, we still would not win," he said. The other meeting was with a CIA officer, not yet totally disillusioned with the war and its conduct but, nevertheless, hobbled by confusion and disenchantment, by the corruption of the military junta he was helping to keep in place and dejected by the ignorance and self-imposed blinders of the State Department and the Pentagon.

109

"They don't even read the cables that do not support the cockeyed idea of the moment," he complained.

The most important mission for the Saigon command during Cronkite's visit was to keep him as secure as possible. He was the last person the State Department wanted to lose. One can imagine the fate of an army escort who had allowed Walter Cronkite, the most trusted man in America, to be captured or killed. Of course three years later, during the Tet Offensive, they did "lose" Cronkite. After his broadcast from Hue, when he suggested that the only rational way out of Vietnam was to negotiate, Lyndon Johnson allegedly said, "If we've lost Cronkite, we've lost the war."

There must be a thousand steps up to the highest of the caves in Marble Mountain. From the base the stairway, rising and twisting, spiraling to the highest pinnacles, has the appearance of a painted backdrop; as if some traveling company of *Lost Horizon* had erected a large canvas mural of the road to Shangri-La. I recall a line from Kipling's *Kim*: "Surely the Gods live here."

The path, carved out of the blue gray stone, switches back and forth, full of false perspectives, a road to some Oriental Babel designed by M. C. Escher. It is only the presence of dozens of children, pushy persistent nine- and ten-year-olds trying to sell carved marble souvenirs, that gives the mountain and the stairway any reality. They swirl around like litters of puppies at feeding time. There are pitifully few potential customers, so each urchin's appeal is more whining than the next. Their goods are quite attractive, but it is all the same stuff, and the effect is to make it all dismissable junk. There are bracelets, necklaces, and earrings; sets of bookends in the form of reclining lions, candlesticks, and elephants; and of course the inevitable Buddhas and Jesuses, angels and fairies, dragons and swastikas and crosses to guard against the evil eye. The evil eye has stared so balefully down on Vietnam for so many centuries, I wonder that they have not come up with some more effective talismans.

There are a series of long broad landings on the walk to the top.

110

At some there are entrances to good-sized caves that have been made into Buddhist pagodas. People lounge around staring at the Buddhas, at us, at the chickens who peck away at bits of mountain shrubbery.

Two thirds of the way up, the path broadens out to a wide courtyard surrounded by carefully kept gardens. At one side is a large shrine leading to a monastery; on the other, a cave entrance with an opening about six feet high and four feet wide. The effect of walking through the entrance is difficult to describe. I feel like Alice or some other character from a children's story. Walk through an innocent doorway and arrive in another country, another state of mind . . . a vast cavern with walls that slope inward and up for a hundred feet or more forming the inside of a steeple, a narrow opening at the top, letting in light, which by the time it has reached the cavern floor, has been filtered and softened to create the effect of light passing through pale green stained glass. At one end is an enormous altar carved out of the solid rock. On all sides are Buddhas, who in this light seem more ghostly than serene. The only noise is the steady trickle of water dropping from the top of the steeple and seeping in small rivulets from the sides.

From the outside there is no hint of this place. There are hundreds of cave openings in this mountain leading to rooms no more than four or five feet square . . . so the shock of discovery is as if I'd opened a door to a motel room and found Notre Dame Cathedral inside.

The place is empty now. It is obvious from the stale offerings on the altar that few pilgrims make the trek. But during the war it was a Vietcong hospital, probably the most secure and best equipped in South Vietnam. Right above one of the largest concentrations of American military power in the world, the enemy recovered from his wounds, well supplied no doubt from the flourishing black market in Danang and the high-grade garbage Americans conveniently create wherever they settle.

As I leave the pagoda to climb down the seaward side of the

111

mountain, I see the main road that led to the old headquarters of the 1st Marine Regiment and wonder what the Vietcong wounded and their doctors must have thought of all that furious activity down below, all that firepower and musclepower, all that backing and forthing of a modern army, with its bureaucracies and channels of communication, chains of command, and business, urgent and otherwise. Were they envious or just amused? In *Brothers in Arms*, Bill Broyles, a former editor of *Newsweek* and a former marine who served just a mile or so away from where I am standing, has written of this place:

> The Viet Cong in the hospital must have heard our trucks, and the helicopters from the airfield every day. . . . No doubt they could listen to the parties at the airfield or China Beach, hear the Filipino bands singing "Proud Mary," and "We Gotta Get Out of This Place."
>
> How little we knew. And our enemy was so certain of our ignorance, so confident we'd learn nothing that he had hidden his hospital in plain sight, like Poe's purloined letter. To be defeated was bad enough. To be treated with such contempt was far worse.

Most of the Buddhist temples in Vietnam were off-limits to GIs. They were briefed to respect the religious sensibilities of the Vietnamese, and generally they did. It was one of the few aspects of the culture that Americans did respect, and at Marble Mountain anyway, one they should have been more curious about. The Buddhist priests in Danang were among the most militant in the country and continuously supported, if not the Vietcong, then at least the vague coalition called "the resistance." In 1966 they led an uprising that spread to the students, the police, and the army that for most of a month virtually suspended the war.

American intelligence was so awful it seemed that no one bothered to read even the travelers' tales, dating back to the eighteenth century and repeated into the twentieth, describing the honeycomb of caves

112

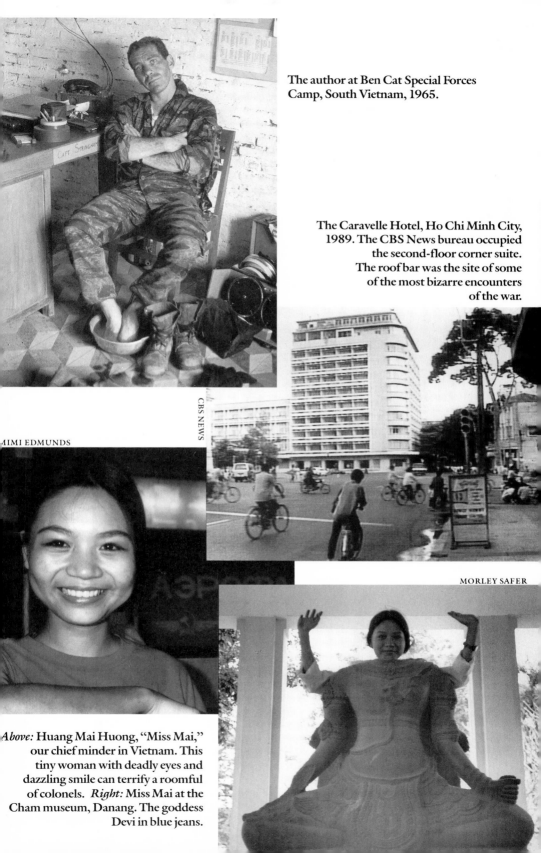

The author at Ben Cat Special Forces Camp, South Vietnam, 1965.

The Caravelle Hotel, Ho Chi Minh City, 1989. The CBS News bureau occupied the second-floor corner suite. The roof bar was the site of some of the most bizarre encounters of the war.

CBS NEWS

MIMI EDMUNDS

MORLEY SAFER

Above: Huang Mai Huong, "Miss Mai," our chief minder in Vietnam. This tiny woman with deadly eyes and dazzling smile can terrify a roomful of colonels. *Right:* Miss Mai at the Cham museum, Danang. The goddess Devi in blue jeans.

General William C. Westmoreland with Charles Collingwood, "the Duke," and the author at Westmoreland's headquarters, December 1966.

The Vietcong colonel who usurped our dinner, well into his cups, well into a harangue against American imperialism. A thorough embarrassment to his Vietnamese and American guests.

Pig in a poke, Danang airport, 1989. The Russians are not amused.

Van Le near Cu Chi, 1989. The former private in the People's Army of Vietnam is now a poet and novelist in Ho Chi Minh City. "Any bullet from wherever it comes is shot at the mother first, not at the son who is killed."

Major Nguyen Be, as hard a man as you will find in Vietnam. During the war he infiltrated the U.S. Marine air base at Danang. As cold blooded as he seems, he confesses that he dreams about the war every night.

General Vo Nguyen Giap, Hanoi, 1989, the legendary commander of Communist forces in both the French and American wars. He says he never went through a moment of doubt, conscience, or pity about sending so many thousands to the slaughter.

Dr. Duong Quynh Hoa, one of the founders of the National Liberation Front, the Vietcong. In 1979, thoroughly disillusioned, she left the party. "Nobody won this war. Nobody."

Professor Nguyen Ngoc Hung, Sgt. (ret.), People's Army of Vietnam, at Trung Son Cemetery. "They were the best sons and daughters of Vietnam."

Colonel Bui Tin, Hanoi, 1989. He was wounded seven times in the wars against the French and the Americans. "When I was seventeen I wanted to go to France and study philosophy, but somehow it never worked out."

Pham Xuan An, former correspondent for *Time* magazine and former colonel in the Vietcong, with the author in Ho Chi Minh City, 1989. The "spy in winter" is a dignified and decent man… a believer still in a small, honorable destiny for his country.

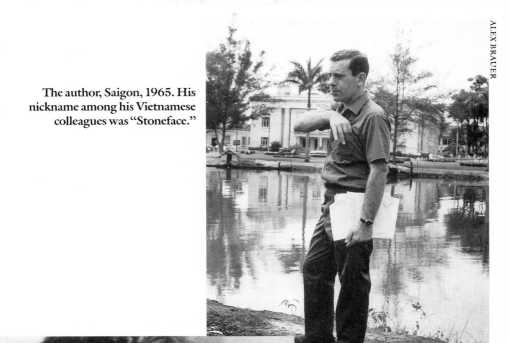

The author, Saigon, 1965. His nickname among his Vietnamese colleagues was "Stoneface."

Tran Thi "Eliza Doolittle" Gung, hero of the revolution. She said of her captive: "They told me Americans were ugly, but he was tall and fair and very handsome."

Mr. Su and Mr. Tu, the "hapless heroes." After fourteen years, still waiting for a check.

The marine search-and-destroy operation in
Cam Ne, August 1965. It was these scenes of
U.S. Marines rousting people from their homes

and then burning most of the village to
the ground that set off a firestorm of
accusations against CBS by the White House.

Bill Baldwin, "Vietnam vet and proud of it," in Ho Chi Minh City, 1989. "Everybody has a sense of unfinished business. I've longed for Vietnam ever since I came home. I dreamed about it. I think when I go home, the chapter will be over."

in the mountains. All through the war it struck me that enlisted men had a better understanding of the place than did the officers and civilians commanding them. Battalion commanders would complain that the Vietcong would not stand up and fight, as if they expected them to play by some book prepared at West Point or Annapolis. Of course, had the people in civilian and military command even the most rudimentary understanding of the history and language, this awful business would likely not have happened.

Half walking, half stumbling down the mountain to China Beach, I hear a faint chorus of tapping that grows louder as sea level is approached. The stonemasons of Danang live surrounded by the raw materials of their craft in shops and rooms hacked out of the mountain's base. Here they tap away at grave markings and at souvenirs, each with a stand offering his best work, tended by more children, mostly girls, but very formal, unlike their cousins on the other side of the mountain. They tend their treasures with such severity and aplomb that they might be offering emeralds at Cartier.

China Beach was perhaps the only place in Vietnam where a restless GI could catch a glimpse of an American woman dressed in something more fetching than fatigues. These men, who were so abusive and presumptuous with Vietnamese women, were reduced to awkward adolescents by the nurses. They would look but would not touch. "Round-eyed" women were viewed as part mother figure, part inaccessible movie goddess. The nurses were also, of course, officers and therefore doubly untouchable. Donut Dollies, the Red Cross volunteers who also visited China Beach, were held in somewhat less awe. There is an appalling television show on ABC-TV called *China Beach*. I have seen it only once. The most gross insult a business enterprise could concoct, it reduces the nurses to randy Barbie dolls or pretentious schoolmarms and the marines to shambling fools or psychopaths. I cannot believe that the same Bill Broyles who wrote *Brothers in Arms* is the "executive consultant" of this enterprise as the credits claim.

113

China Beach is practically deserted. A few children are playing in the surf, others are gathering seaweed. Stands here and there are selling sickly sweet lemonade and coconuts, the milk of which is served in glasses that have not been washed since the marines landed. I look back at Marble Mountain hovering above with its look of make-believe. It really is a Chinese landscape painting in the sense that the great masters did not paint from life but from the imagination. The Chinese words for landscape are nothing more than "water and mountain."

Morley Safer

15

"Street Without Joy"

4:00 P.M.: The road back to Danang is a section of the old French colonial Route 1, the national road that runs from Saigon practically to the Chinese border. During the French war, Highway 1 was a graveyard for military convoys. The French were picked to pieces by Viet Minh ambushes, and the stretch of road near Hue became known as the Street Without Joy. Bernard Fall, a French journalist and scholar, used the phrase for the title of his classic book on Vietnam, published in 1961. It dealt with the inability of the American-equipped French colonial army either to defend itself or to seek out Viet Minh sanctuaries. His book—all seven of his books—are primers in counterinsurgency. I got to know Bernie quite well in the sixties. He lived in Washington but was a fixture in Saigon. *Street Without Joy* was required reading for American infantry commanders, and even though the Pentagon hated Fall for his constant criticism of tactics, it used him as an unofficial consultant.

Officers would quote him in the officers' club, then go out and

115

repeat the mistakes the French made in the field. I always had the feeling that they read his books as adventure stories rather than as the cautionary tales he intended.

Bernie Fall was a large man with unquenchable enthusiasms and an ego to match. I once told him that I'd noticed all his books stacked on a senior general's desk. He reached into his shoulder bag and pulled out his reviews, all of them raves, and started reading them out loud.

He was a most unlikely-looking scholar, dressed in either shorts and shirt open to the navel or combat boots and army fatigues, the many pockets of which were stuffed with notebooks, paperbacks, copies of his own books, and a half-dozen pens of different colors. Regardless of the light, he wore heavily tinted glasses that made him look slightly sinister.

As much time as he spent in Vietnam, in the field with the French and then with the Americans, as much time as he spent studying the minutiae of Vietnamese politics, lecturing at Howard University, consulting to the U.S. government, he never grew weary of the subject. He had an adolescent's enthusiasm for the details. He could quote statistics from obscure ambushes the way other men remember batting averages. Yet unlike many journalists and others who became obsessed with Vietnam, he was not a war lover.

Hawks and doves both used his material, or at least selected quotations, to prove their points. He was accused by the military command in Saigon of having a defeatist attitude, but the officers read every book, every article he wrote. As much as they read, they never grasped his single most important point—that the peasant soldiers of the South, unlike their Vietcong cousins, had no ideology to die for, no leader to follow, and only rich naïve interlopers to prod them into fighting a war using tactics that had been discredited a generation earlier.

The last time I saw him was in late February 1967. I had just completed my second tour in Vietnam and was leaving for good, or so I thought. Over lunch I told him that I felt there was nothing more to tell about this place; it had all been reported over and over again. I was sour on the story, and I should have been gone by New Year's, but New York had asked me to stay on and write and produce a one-hour documentary, *A Last Letter Home*.

"And I do mean last," I said.

"You'll be back," he said. "This place gets in the blood."

Fall was in his usual state of excitement and self-aggrandizement. His latest book, *Hell in a Very Small Place*, a painstakingly detailed .account of the French defeat at Dien Bien Phu, had just been published in New York to spectacular reviews and was an even bigger hit in Saigon.

He was dressed in fatigues and carrying a shoulder bag.

"Where are you going?" I asked.

"To Danang, there are some marine operations going on that I want to take a look at. That, after all, is my country they're tramping around in."

I was scheduled to leave on the afternoon flight to Hong Kong, and I offered him a lift to the military side of Tan Son Nhut Airport, where he could hitch a ride to Danang.

When he got out of the car we shook hands, and he said again: "You'll be back; I promise you."

We both laughed, then I tried to get serious.

"Why are you doing this; what are you trying to prove? What are you going to learn on yet another walk in the sun? You're a full professor, for chrissake."

"It's the only way I can work . . . besides it's expected of me . . . to give long detailed accounts of how the Americans are fucking up even worse than we French did."

I caught my flight to Hong Kong, lingered for a day or two, and went on to New York to finish writing the Vietnam hour. I had just settled into an office in the CBS Special Events unit, when Richard Kallsen, a CBS News radio editor, walked in with some wire copy in his hand.

"You were a friend of Fall's, weren't you?"

117

"Yes . . . what do you mean 'were'?"

"He's dead . . . he was on a marine patrol . . . stepped on a land mine. Will you do the obit . . . no more than a minute please." When Kallsen passed me the wire copy, he looked slightly apologetic. We were both perfectly aware of the limited time available to deceased military historians.

When he was killed, Fall had all the paperwork ready to apply for American citizenship. It would have been his third. He was born in Vienna, fled to Paris with his parents as refugees, and spent the last few years of the Second World War in the French Resistance. The French government gave him a medal for his efforts. He was a restless man, full of ambition, a kind of scholarly Sammy Glick. He was contemptuous of academics and journalists who wrote about Vietnam from the intellectual and physical safety of Washington. His enormous ego hid, I suppose, a certain lack of self-confidence. He always said he wanted to be considered the most distinguished military writer of his generation. When he went out with the marines that day, he'd already achieved it. Perhaps he was the only one who was not entirely certain.

He was killed fourteen miles from Hue, smack in the middle of "his country," just a few hundred yards from the Street Without Joy. He was born, curiously, on November 11, Armistice Day. He was only forty when he died.

He was right: I did go back to Vietnam, twice more during the war . . . and now back again, driving along Highway 1, the street that Bernie Fall and all those other corpses made famous.

It is as joyless as it ever was, but no longer in the heavy-on-the-irony French way, no longer a snipers-and-sappers delight. It is a different sadness—an emptiness, a slight case of the postrevolutionary blues.

Today it crosses a barren plain of sand and scrub pine. Twenty years ago it was impossible to know what life or absence of life existed beyond the asphalt, for both shoulders stood high with seagoing

118

containers, trailers, trucks just abandoned there or still laden with pallets of the necessities of modern warfare. Beans and bullets is the phrase old soldiers use to describe such goods. The Vietnam list included hairspray and deodorant; Coke, Pepsi, and Budweiser cans by the billion; all the makings of "Po-Boy" sandwiches; and millions of vials of cure for the clap. It was not called the clap or even gonorrhea, to spare the feelings of parents and wives back home. It was known simply as NSU—Nonspecific Urethritis, more common in Vietnam than the common cold.

Whatever space there was along the roadside had been taken up by squatters, refugees from the free-fire zones that the marines had designated all around Danang. They lived in what the French call Bidonvilles, tin-can cities, little urban blights that can be found on the edges of every former colonial city in Africa and Asia. The houses are made, literally, of tin cans flattened and wired together and then nailed to a scrap-wood frame. The roof was of corrugated iron begged, stolen, or cast away from one military-industrial complex or another. There had been a Bidonville covering twenty acres on the outskirts of Algiers during the civil war and a sister slum in Paris housing Arab refugees who carried French passports.

Bidonvilles were my first experience of effective recycling. Vietnamese craftsmen were quick to capitalize on the GI fascination with the uses of American garbage. Thousands went back to "the world" with sets of matching Budweiser luggage. Junior staff officers tended to be more discreet and carry the colonel's papers in a slim Coke or Pepsi attaché case.

For three or four miles Highway 1 slides past nothing, then to the left, to the west, a low concrete wall begins and continues for a mile or more. Over the top of it, discernible, familiar shapes slip by; the fuselage and tail rotor of a helicopter, tank treads piled high, the broken arm of an olive drab backhoe, mountains of enormous rubber tires. As we pass a set of gates set into the wall, I ask the driver to stop, to turn around, and to pull into the place. Behind the iron

119

gates two men in hard hats shout and gesture to us that we are not welcome, that photography is prohibited, and that in any case they are about to close and would we kindly leave.

I tell Miss Mai that I would like to go in and look around. She produces her magic pass, which has absolutely no effect. She flashes that blinding smile, still nothing. She says something, a short sharp chop in Vietnamese, and crosses the road to a small cottage. Minutes later she returns looking quite pleased with herself. Beside her, a man in his fifties, clearly the manager, is trotting along making twittering sounds. He orders the hard hats to open the gates and makes us welcome. Hanoi once again triumphs over the South.

Inside is a graveyard, a boot hill of war junk. There are acres of it. Thousands of artillery shell casings, steel reinforcing rods, and U.S. Air Force buses and refueling trucks. It is also the resting place of all those steel shipping containers that once lined the roadside. A steel helmet with neat entry and exit wounds rests on the lip of an abandoned bulldozer blade.

Jeeps or parts of jeeps are scattered across the entire landscape. There was a time when it seemed that every South Vietnamese above the rank of sergeant was supplied with his own jeep by the United States, and rarely were they driven to war. The streets of Danang and Saigon were clogged with them, each filled with families who seemed to be going on outings of one kind or another. War may well be an exercise in waste. In this war it seemed to be its sole point. To test the resourcefulness of the CBS News contact at the Saigon black market, the supplier of all our fatigues, boots, flak jackets, and C rations, I once asked him if he could supply me with a tank.

"No problem. Maybe one week. You want APC [armored personnel carrier]? I get right now."

I walk past the ranks of dead machinery with the manager, reading off manufacturers' labels from Michigan, Ohio, and Tennessee, and wonder what the enemy must have made of all the ingenious contraptions we dumped on this war. Trucks and tanks and artillery pieces, simple. But a pizza oven? And all those steel desks. Why on earth so many desks?

The manager explains that this is the last of the scrap from the Danang area, that most of it has already been shipped out.

"Where?"

"The Japanese ships come every month. They take it back to Japan and melt it down. I don't know what they do with it after that."

I do. After a little alchemy, it finds its way home in the shapes of Toyotas and Hondas. In Connecticut I keep a Nissan pickup truck. What was it in its previous life? A piece of the helicopter I was in that was shot down in the battle of the Ia Drang Valley? A part of that APC that blew up near Cu Chi? Maybe it's the ghost of the old CBS jeep in Danang that expired long before the war did. The Japanese should be made to give the provenance of their vehicles. It would be nice to know.

It is getting dark, the soft smoky Asian night is coming on. The rust, the olive drab, the camouflage splatters on all this wreckage fade to a common blackness forming dark fantastic silhouettes against the evening sky. I feel filled up with a terrible sadness. Nothing of us remains, except the decay of this colossal wreck, boundless and bare. Ozymandias in camouflage paint. Which desk held the treasures of that safari-suited Foreign Service officer who mouthed on about hearts and minds and was thinking R and R? Which one belonged to the moronic colonel who hired Vietnamese craftsmen to carve into mahogany for him conversation pieces like "Take them firmly by the balls and their hearts and minds will follow" and "Join the Marines! Travel to exotic lands . . . meet exciting unusual people . . . and kill them."

Shelley would have wept. Not at our brutality or even our ambition. Just at the tragic foolishness of it all.

16

"Something Good Is Going to Happen to You Today"

Danang, January 24, 5:00 A.M.:   I rise early to go for a prebreakfast unattended walk through Danang. The schedule is so tight there is little time for reflection or observation, no time to get lost and discover some small truth about this place or that. The early hours are the best time to see a Southeast Asian city. To watch it wake up and get on with its life.

The streets are rich with the smell of charcoal smoke from a thousand fires warming up the pots of morning soup. Everywhere there are small points of light from candles and oil lamps and cooking fires. The endless Asian cavalcade rolls by, a woman carrying water from a public spigot, the steady flow of cycle traffic going one way, the gray-backed river flowing the other . . . people squatting in doorways and stalls, faces splashed with lamplight . . . a man on his haunches straining in the half-light to read one People's daily or another. Another peeing against a wall not so discreetly as he thinks. A poor family in almost regal procession strolls by barefoot, splay-

Morley Safer

footed . . . husband in front with little boy in hand, the wife next with infant on her hip, another child taking up the rear, barely old enough to walk, wearing a shift that falls way short of her bare bottom. She turns and stares blankly at me, at this hairy-armed harmless alien. The food stalls open for business. The stench of durian takes command; that Southeast Asian fruit that, the worse it smells, the better it tastes. The feeling of life, of early morning optimism, is almost palpable.

Around some corner, no doubt, the local offices of various ministries are waking up, ready to begin their dreary business of typing and filing, duplicating and stamping, putting callers, and life, on hold.

The streets and the countryside seem totally unaffected by it. The bureaucratic ship sails one way; the people drift somewhere else on currents all their own. It was the same under the French, the Diems, and the barely disguised American colonial rule. And it is the same today under the Hanoi bureaucrats.

I find my way back to the Phuong Dong Hotel. As I pack for the return trip to Ho Chi Minh City I turn on my shortwave radio, vainly seeking the BBC overseas service. All I can find is a selection of American evangelists who hammer away at godless Asia from relay stations in southern India, the Seychelles, and the Maldive Islands. As I go down to breakfast Oral Roberts, the younger, reminds me that "something *Good*, something *Really Good* is going to happen to you . . . *today*!"

It is not yet eight when Miss Mai advises me that the plane to Ho Chi Minh City has been delayed, for possibly as much as two hours. One of the delights of primitive travel in Asian backwaters is the easy access to accurate information. Computers have not yet rotted the brains of the young and the clerical. So a phone call to Danang Airport actually produces facts, and travelers are spared the melancholy curse of the lifetime wait in an airport lounge.

The delay is an opportunity to see Danang unencumbered by darkness, camera crews, or minders. With Patti Hassler, I head for the market. Everywhere in Vietnam, especially in the South, people mark their lives from the 1986 Communist Party Congress decision to decentralize the economy. The result in Danang is a building spree, an attempt it seems to turn every one-story dwelling into a two-story business dwelling. The country is much too poor to afford modern building materials, but the Vietnamese, ever-practical hoarders of anything with a potential use, somehow manage to build fairly decent extensions using homemade mud bricks, scrap wood from the remains of American military installations, sheets of corrugated iron, and straw mats reinforced with cane. By a curbside a child squats next to a five-foot pile of bent nails of varying sizes. He lays each one on a brick and carefully straightens it, rolling it over, gently tapping it with a piece of iron pipe.

As inventive as it all seems, none of this would be happening without that Vietnamese sixth sense, foresight. In even the most optimistic days of the war, the South Vietnamese had little belief in either their government or the American commitment to shore it up.

I cannot think of a single Vietnamese friend who had any belief that the South would win or continue to exist after a truce. Like their leaders, they salted away dollars, gold, anything negotiable. The people of the streets, unlike their leaders, had little opportunity to stash it overseas. They buried it in mattresses and back gardens and tucked it into family shrines.

One soaking night in 1967 near Duc Co I sat up talking with an overage paratroop major named Phuong. He was well into his fifties, spoke good French and English, had served in the French army in Vietnam and then in Algeria, and was now back fighting his third war. A gallant and unselfish man, resigned to the fact that sooner or later he would lay down his life for a cause he had no belief in, for generals who were cowards or criminals. Bui Tin, the North Vietnamese colonel who took the surrender of Saigon, could have been his twin.

"The choice is so simple," Phuong said. "My courageous commanders keep sending me to places like Duc Co, trying to get me killed, and the VC want to kill me. It is a thrilling life . . . to be paid seventy-five dollars a month in piasters for such interesting work. I feel lucky. My men have not been paid for three months. I hope Madam Thieu is investing their money wisely."

A shopkeeper in Saigon told me in 1966: "Supporting this government makes me feel ashamed of myself and my country—such wonderful choices are open to us. The Communists want to take the little I have. But they respect my existence as a Vietnamese. The people in the president's palace have only contempt for me.

"I have my little treasury of green money for that awful great day that will surely come. Unlike some others, I will not fly the Communist flag, and I will not run away. I will wait in my shop."

He did not survive the war. He died of cancer a month before Saigon fell. I have no idea what happened to his treasury, but here in Danang there seems to be evidence of everyone else's hard at work.

The market has doubled in size since the war, and if you were to see only this place, you might be deceived into believing that Vietnam is a prosperous country. The effect of the decision to allow land to be held almost privately is a devastating indictment of Marxist theology. The stalls are piled high with produce that would be proudly displayed in Balducci's in New York, Fortnum & Mason in London, or Fauchon in Paris. Carrots and shallots, spring onions, broad beans with a green sheen on them as if each had been simonized . . . stall after stall of Oriental mystery vegetables and more familiar beets, celery, radishes, and garlic as fat and hippy as the best of Provence. In the delicacy section, old Jim Beam bourbon bottles have been recycled to hold an array of differently spiced *nuoc mam,* that glorious Vietnamese essence of fish and a variety of red pepper sauces. Everything is offered to taste by black-toothed market hags. All very jolly and slightly, I suspect, salacious in their invitations. The fish market gleams with shark and something that looks like sea bass and something that looks like mullet and something else that looks

125

like yellowtail. There are live chickens and ducks and an open-air butcher's stall selling slabs of beef and pork. This, like all Third World meat markets and some First World butcher shops, should, at all costs, be avoided.

There are beautifully made baskets and artfully patterned rush carpets and a stall that sells slabs of exotic wood for chopping boards, each one a slice cut from the trunk of a tree.

All these riches, I later learn, were displayed within weeks of the Party Congress. The moment it was reported that individual enterprise was to be encouraged, every peasant, every person with even the most minor of skills, went berserk with capitalism.

It is a deceptive display of wealth. It takes so many worthless dong to buy a decent meal that I cannot imagine who can afford any of this produce. I suspect the engine of economic life is barter, for, while there are thousands of homeless people, there are very few beggars, and I have rarely seen hunger.

The signs of poverty and shortages are occasionally madcap. One of the legacies of central planning is an absence of paper or plastic products of any kind. Thus, even the most insignificant purchase, a box of tea, a bunch of onions, is presented by the shopkeeper in a handsome, hand-crafted straw bag, whose value in a cash economy would be double or triple that of the goods placed in it.

All along the outer rim of the market a hundred or so small entrepreneurs have established themselves in kiosks, behind old school desks, or simply on a blanket placed on the pavement. A man's life could be tended to on this rectangular stroll . . . a repairer of prosthetic devices occupies a school desk . . . then a man selling faucets, new and used . . . a woman about to begin a fry-up of dumplings . . . next to a watch and clock repairman, a woman has established herself in what looks to be an old popcorn cart. The glass encasement is filled with eyeglasses of every description. She buys and sells and she repairs with a set of jeweler's tools neatly displayed on a swatch of fraying velvet. She is very precise in her movements,

126

picking up and replacing each instrument exactly in its proper place. She performs her task with the intensity of a microsurgeon. I stand and watch for a moment. She looks up and points out that both arms of my sunglasses are so limp that the entire frame is in danger of coming apart. I offer them for repair, which she does with a few dainty flicks of the wrist and then offers them back. They feel practically new; they are so firm, and somehow in the few seconds she had them she managed to polish the lenses as well. I offer her payment, which she refuses, then a pack of cigarettes, which, surprisingly, she also declines. This good-natured confrontation attracts a small friendly crowd, which gets friendlier when a young, very serious looking man, perhaps eighteen years old, explains that we are not Russians. He asks me in French that is clear but suffering a severe case of the Vietnamese glottals, what we are doing in Danang. I answer in French that is clear but suffering from an equally severe case of the Canadian nasals, that I have returned to Vietnam for the purpose of a television broadcast.

"Oh, the war," he says.

"Yes, the war," I reply. "You are too young to remember it. I suppose you've learned about it in school."

"A little. And my uncle told me about it . . . but it is not part of my curriculum. I am studying to be an engineer. Do you have any French books?"

Again, the American war is such a minor part of these peoples' lives, especially the young ones. And again the hunger for anything to read.

"Why French?" I ask him. I am surprised that he is not studying Russian, which many of the younger, educated Vietnamese, I've been told, were eager to learn.

"The school used to make us learn Russian, but we have great difficulty with it. Two years ago they started English and French. Russian is useless for an engineer. But I hope to go to Russia, to the Foreign Language Institute, to learn to speak French perfectly."

127

It must be a little frustrating for Vietnam's only genuine ally to witness its friendship and largesse, as limited as both have been, shrugged off with such indifference.

As we wait in front of the hotel for transport to the airport, the usual gang of eight- and ten-year-old street children swirls around us trying to cadge cigarettes, pennies, chocolates, or even a word or two of banter. Among them, one stands out. He is a pitiful outcast, suffering from some skin affliction or recovering from a beating. He is taller than the rest, flaxen haired, with the face of a Tartar, and skin, at least the undamaged parts of it, the color of parchment. This offspring of some alleyway embrace by a Soviet adviser is part of Vietnam's new breed of unwanted. The Amerasians, the half-American afterthoughts, are now in adolescence or older. The big-shouldered cold warriors have taken their turns with Vietnam, joining the queue as in some small-town whorehouse. The boy stares blankly at us, not noticing the shoves and elbows that force him to the outside of the circle of children.

Morley Safer

17

Pig in a Poke

11:00 A.M.: At the airport a plane arrives bearing Russians, families based at the huge Soviet-Vietnamese naval base at Cam Ranh Bay. The base is off-limits to most foreigners. Cam Ranh is supposed to be strategically the most important deep-water port in Asia, and the story is told that Ho Chi Minh once offered the United States a permanent base there in exchange for American support for his resistance to the French. It is one of the popular legends of Southeast Asia and is regularly trotted out by peaceniks and hindsight cynics to demonstrate how easily the war could have been avoided.

As for the Russians, not a single one, male or female, weighs in under two hundred forty pounds. Each face is beet red, the Russian skin does not take to tanning. Not a smile graces the lips of even one of them. The women are wearing housedresses, enormous floral sacks that, on these lumpy damp bodies, become form-fitting. Each woman is clutching a handbag of black imitation leather and carrying a shopping bag filled with *ao dais,* the double-slit full-length dress and pantaloons that traditional-minded women in Vietnam still wear.

129

The *ao dai* is fitted tight around the waist and over the hips and makes these slim, fragilely constructed women even more willowy. A street filled with them, their hair falling down their backs to their waists, the way it is worn in Hue, is a remarkable sight. The swaying hair, glistening black in the sun, the gentle flapping of the *ao dais* make the street shimmer, as if seen through a heat haze. I once wrote a poem about such a moment. Mercifully I have both lost and forgotten it.

I imagine the fashion show on some Saturday-night-to-come in Omsk or Novosibirsk. I can only think of Queen Celeste, wife of Babar, king of the elephants, togging up for a tea party, forgoing her normal pink polka dot for one of these Oriental numbers. The Russians grow large in a way that seems totally different from other nationalities. There is no soft roundness to them; it is more like layer upon layer of armor-plated elephant hide.

The men are wearing T-shirts that leave a two-inch gap of belly on display. The tight shirts are sweated through, and for some reason most of them are emblazoned with Fuji Color with, for variety, a few Coke symbols and one I ♥ New York. They clink and clank as they gather in front of the terminal. Their shopping bags are filled with bottles of vodka and bottles of cobra tonic.

Vietnamese men, regardless of age, class, or education, believe in the aphrodisiac powers of cobra tonic. It is, quite literally, snake oil. The cheapest is made of a single cobra fermented in a cocktail of various oils and juices. The most expensive and most potent include the essences of three different types of poisonous snake, filtered and aged in alcohol. I have not yet found a need for cobra tonic, although time and nature, those twin destroyers of passion, may soon tempt me to make the taste test. Paul Oppenheim, the sound engineer for this enterprise, bought a case of cobra tonic to take home to California, where, if it works at all, it will endanger the entire snake population of the American West. Professor Hung, a firm believer, told me: "Don't drink it if you are trying to concentrate on some work. It can have a very distracting effect."

130

I scan the airport looking for my beautiful *douanier,* to perhaps get a second opinion, but she is nowhere to be found. Up above, as we wait for the plane to Ho Chi Minh City, a pair of MiG-23s are playing follow the leader . . . low-level passes over the main strip, then powering up into a steep climb. They pierce the high cloud cover, and Danang Airport goes utterly silent.

This was once the noisiest place in Vietnam. Beyond the jet screams, there was the continuous din of the more peaceable business of war; the surf sound of air conditioners from the contractors' trailers, the blasts from the air horns of Vietnamese Army trucks. Vietnamese drivers use the horn as a kind of mechanical mantra. But all is dead silence now, all sound muffled by the shroud of heat rising from the pavement.

The silence is broken by the harsh squeaking sound of a bicycle badly in need of a grease job. It is being pedaled by a man in his early twenties who is wearing flared trousers, flip-flops on his feet, and on his head, oddly, what looks to be a ski cap.

His passenger is an enormous pig. It has been stuffed head first into a conical straw basket and the whole package tied onto the back carrier of the bike. The pig's rump and tail are hanging limply out of the open end. A grandmotherly woman approaches the pig and gives it a few good prods on its backside and proceeds to bargain with the cyclist. I feel as if I have walked onto the set of a Jacques Tati movie as the scene is darkened for a moment by the shadow of the Air Vietnam turboprop as it comes in low for its landing. The pig stares out of its see-through poke with a look of sad acceptance of its predicament. The Russians stare back stonily, neither amusement nor curiosity crossing their faces.

Except for two of the men: two drunks who are swigging from the same bottle. They are not enjoying this little rustic moment; they are mocking it with coarse, profane noises. Perhaps because they do so little of it, Russians make terrible travelers and are, as imperial envoys, even worse than Americans. They roam the less-developed world tending aid and engineering projects with open contempt for

131

anything non-Russian. Even the smallest gesture of sympathy or curiosity seems out of their reach.

Privately they may display ordinary human acts of tenderness, but en masse, like this airport gang, crudeness seems to be the accepted form.

Peter Ustinov, that chameleon of an actor and semiprofessional apologist for all things Russian, including expansionism, bad manners, arrogance, and aggressive paranoia, once told me that it is merely a matter of misunderstood facial expressions, voice, and posture. That if we could look behind these brutish façades, we would find the true gentility of these people.

Ustinov explained this as we walked through Red Square in Moscow, and to make his point, he transformed his face and body into an aging half-pissed Leonid Brezhnev. The crowd of Russians in the square went into shock. Brezhnev had been dead for three years, but for a moment they were aghast, almost convinced that the old thief had managed to squirm out of his casket. This is a very Russian kind of fear. The poet Yevgeny Yevtushenko expressed such a fear of Stalin coming back in "The Heirs of Stalin": "the coffin smolders slightly, through its chinks, breath percolates. . . ."

I cannot imagine a life haunted by familiar monsters . . . of sharing a collective history of self-loathing that seems to be almost genetically instilled. No wonder it turns them into lousy travelers and drives them to drink, poetry, and other forms of madness.

When the flight for Ho Chi Minh City is announced, the Russians gather together as a single unit and troop across the tarmac. The Vietnamese passengers, as ever, race for the plane's steps. All the careful explanation that the number of boarding passes exactly matches the number of seats does nothing to convince a Vietnamese traveler that he or she will actually get on the plane. I have seen these otherwise thoughtful and formal people knock down ancient grannies in their sprint for an airplane's steps. During the war I put it down to the Air Vietnam ticket sellers' racket of demanding bribes in exchange for a guaranteed place. In today's Vietnam travel is so thoroughly controlled, there is no need for this Oklahoma seat rush. But bad habits die hard.

The flight to Ho Chi Minh City lasts just under two hours, but it seems like six. They have managed to cram at least half a dozen rows of extra seats in these planes on the assumption, no doubt, that the Vietnamese are small in stature and bottom. The seats are so narrow and so close together that Western travelers do not so much take their seats as plug themselves into them . . . like a cork into a bottle. In the slight chop during the descent to Tan Son Nhut a few of the Vietnamese passengers discreetly throw up in the paper sick-bags provided. A few Russians do the same, but not so neatly and with a loud chorus of curses from their seatmates. The rising odor of a big-city drunk tank on a Saturday night drifts through the plane. At last it lands and comes to a stop in front of the terminal. In a cold sweat and gasping for air, I lead the rush. But the Vietnamese hang back. They are grabbing for the unused sick bags.

Is there a symbolic significance to the paper shortage? Is there some Parkinson's Law that states that countries that use economic theories that work only on paper are the first to run short of it?

Back at the Majestic, we assemble in the lobby for one of those aching conferences that are the plague of television journalism. The full caravan is there: the six CBS people, plus three drivers, plus Miss Mai, plus two local Ho Chi Minh City minders. It is a collective that at any one time moves and thinks in twelve different directions and has twelve subagendas, at least three cases of dysentery, and one person missing. I have seen television documentary producers driven to threats of murder by a soundman napping unseen in the back of a van . . . or by an amorous driver who has taken off with the car and the cameras to tend to the needs of a friend in the next county— or, in Central America, the next country.

The correspondent generally is a reasonably docile sort—on time,

133

with only a few minor complaints, and willing to go along with some very silly enterprises.

Eric Sevareid, in welcoming me to CBS News twenty-five years ago, described the relationship between producer and correspondent as that between dog and tree: "They never feel they really own you until they've pissed on you," he said in his typically well-turned way.

The group in the Majestic is quite well behaved. Patti Hassler has managed to instill a boot-camp mentality with us all, which means we will stand at attention or, at the very least, wait in place until asked to do otherwise. I ask for and receive permission to take the rest of the afternoon off. I want to visit the Caravelle Hotel, my former home and office.

18

Nil Carborundum in the Jerome et Juliet

Ho Chi Minh City, 2:00 P.M.: Hotels have been a central fact of my life. Some of them—the Aletti in Algiers, the Ledra Palace in Cyprus, the Semiramis in Cairo, the Federal Palace in Lagos, the American Colony in Jerusalem, the Kempinski in Berlin—induce hilarious or chilling images. Each is a discreet neutral island in its own violent sea. There are a thousand more less distinctive motels and hotels that form a blur on the horizon of memory.

As I walk toward the Caravelle it occurs to me that something is missing. Beyond the obvious absences of war, some small visual symbol has disappeared. I stare at the hotel's rounded ugly façade. It has not changed. No floors added; no architectural flourishes. Air France still occupies the ground floor. Across the road, the Continental Palace is boarded up, being renovated, I am told, by an international consortium. The Opera House is intact. The brutal-looking war memorial to the South Vietnamese paratroops is gone . . . but I knew that had been torn down in the first few days of

135

so-called liberation. I once again stare at the Caravelle, at the corner window of the second floor that was the CBS suite, and next to it the room that I had booked for a month and had lived in on and off for three years. It finally strikes me. The tape is missing. All down Tu Do, the antiblast Scotch strapping tape has been removed. In theory the tape would stop plate glass from shattering, and instead of being hit by a thousand small shards, in the event of a bomb blast, the victim would receive the same volume of glass but held together by the genius of the 3M Corporation.

In the lobby of the Caravelle there is not a single familiar face. The front desk was once the domain of a Chinese gentleman who retained the tradition of allowing the nail on his right pinkie to grow to a length of three or four inches. He also maintained a single whisker that hung perhaps two feet from his chin. He could do magical things with that fingernail . . . count thousands of thousand piaster notes with a mere flick of it . . . use it as a surgical instrument for various ear and nose dysfunctions, and when not engaged in any of these, he would allow it to stroke that single black shimmering hair waving from his chin. Both hair and nail seemed to have lives of their own.

The young woman behind the desk tells me that the corner suite, number 206, is occupied, as is my old room adjoining it. "But please go up, the resident may allow you in."

Upstairs there is no answer in either room. The floor boy trots toward me, his sandals flapping on the tile floor, his uniform as white and stiffly starched as in what the Vietnamese now sometimes call "bygone days." I use the colonial term in describing him as the "floor boy," the man is, after all, in his sixties. But "floor attendant" or some other such attempt at an inoffensive locution fails to capture accurately the colonial spirit that still pervades the place.

"This Hungarish embassy," he says, "no home, no home."

He squats on the floor eyeing me fishily, wondering perhaps if I represent some new potential tenant for his corridor of Vietnam. I wonder what these Magyars are making of life on the Mekong. Their absence from the embassy in the middle of the day suggests they've already fallen into that corrupting embrace that seems to be the fate of all comers here. During the war the Australian embassy kept a corner suite, a twin of our bureau, on one of the upper floors of the Caravelle. Each week the entire staff, including the ambassador, could be found across the road at Johnny's, the Indian news agent who would exchange their American dollars for piasters at black-market rates. *Time* and *Newsweek* were the only things ever purchased at Johnny's. The shelves were filled with such journals as *The Basics of Welding* and volumes two and five of *Physics for Beginners.*

Behind a beaded curtain, Johnny must have kept enough bank notes to fill a room. Every month or so the National Police would take him away for a day or two . . . but he always returned, looking ever more dour as the price of maintaining his principles of free trade continued to rise.

He and the other Indian merchants operated the consumer end of a banking system that was owned by Chinese merchants in Cholon. My canceled checks, drawn on the First National City Bank of New York, would come back having been cleared in Hong Kong with the endorsement of a Mr. Hang On. I was never sure if there was such a person or if this was some message from the heart of a gentleman who feared the war would end and business disappear. Once, along with Jack Langguth, then of *The New York Times,* now a professor at the University of Southern California in Los Angeles, I tried to change money at the official, legal rate. The teller at the National Bank of Vietnam looked at us with disbelief. To complete the transaction he dug into his own pocket rather than use the bank's money. "A receipt," asked Langguth. "Of course, of course . . . it is easy to give you a receipt . . . and please anytime you want to change money, you come to me. Please come to me."

At the Caravelle I continue to wait for a Hungarian to turn up. The floor boy and I stare at each other. His face now has the empty

137

friendliness that is the first duty of a professional hotelier, from manager to busboy. It seems that the "Hungarish" have taken the day, or the month, off. I wonder if Budapest is aware that its envoys have succumbed so easily to the sloth that is supposed to afflict only the imperialists. My father would enjoy this. As a sergeant major in the forces of the Austro-Hungarian empire, he, too, had trouble finding Hungarians when he needed them.

I give up my vigil and take the elevator to the top of the Caravelle.

I am pleased to find the elevator car has been replaced. The groaning French tortoise has given way to a silent Japanese hare that fairly leaps to the top of the building. Pleased, not by the technical wizardry, but by the disappearance of the evidence of my crime. Practically my last act in Vietnam seventeen years ago was an act of theft in this very elevator shaft. Leaving for the airport I unscrewed the chromed brass button plate that indicated the hotel floors, from the *rez-de-chaussée* to the Jerome et Juliet bar on the roof. It is the only trophy I took from Vietnam. I felt so awful about it that a few days later I gave it away. Today it graces the wall of a house on the Upper East Side of New York.

The romantic Jerome et Juliet now bears the utilitarian designation of Roof Bar. Except for a paint job it is unchanged. The barman of twenty years ago is still here. He is a man in his sixties who responds to my request for a whiskey and soda in a cold and professional manner. His eyes stare through me as he offers the drink. Not even the slightest nod of recognition. A single table is occupied by four East Germans and two Vietnamese who appear to be officials of some kind. A deal is being transacted in that incongruous manner of the Third World in which the guests, the East Germans, play the relaxed and comfortable hosts and the Vietnamese act the nervous and innocent strangers.

This is the accepted form when West meets Africa or Asia, whether the attaché cases are stuffed with documents confirming the gift or

138

loan of food or money or the construction of a plant to assemble blue jeans or transistor radios is only being proposed.

I get the distinct feeling that somehow all the gentlemen at the table behind me will profit from their transaction at least as much as will their respective fraternal states. There may be have and have-not nations; there is no such thing as a have-not foreign trade bureaucrat.

They all rise in a flurry of handshaking. The East Germans are very jolly. In noisy English they promise the Vietnamese that only good will come of this meeting, while at the same time they seem to be whispering something quite different to each other in German.

When they leave the barman rises from his corner perch and turns down the volume on the tape deck. Diana Ross and the Supremes are just handing over to Sergeant Pepper's Lonely Hearts Club Band.

With the room empty he offers me a bare flicker of acknowledgment. A small tight smile and a few muttered words recalling a livelier time.

This was never a raucous place. It was more like a club than a neighborhood bar. Pentagon generals and certain congressmen accused us of covering the war from here. Their source for this piece of intelligence was a press section story ordered by Henry Luce in *Time* in September 1963. The publisher felt that both the war and its reporting were going badly and accused the press of never leaving this bar and its incestuous relationships. The publisher's reward was the alienation of some of his best correspondents. Selected congressmen and military officers would also occasionally drop in, flown over by the Pentagon to see for themselves. They were accompanied usually by eager young war planners from the State and Defense Departments. Not so much David Halberstam's "best and brightest," as Mary McCarthy's "pale fish out of university think tanks."

139

With few exceptions, visitors behaved well here, although not so well down below on Tu Do Street, where they would put to the test the motto of the Military Assistance Command, that with Vietnamese women, it "was like screwing mice." They would return home, their bodies shot up with antibiotics, their brains fogged by statistics, and their arms laden with ceramic elephants—each a reward for devoted service.

The worst behaved of the six-day experts was the former senator from Arizona, Barry Goldwater.

In 1965, perhaps as some sort of consolation prize for his loss of the presidential election the year before, Goldwater and his wife were given a carefully guided tour of the war. I came up here for a drink about eleven o'clock on their last night in the country. The first-lady-never-to-be sat mesmerized by drink or her husband's wit. The president-who-never-was was holding forth, roaring forth, in his carefully crafted manner—a bush league Harry Truman.

"I'd like to see you pansy reporters out there in the boondocks getting your asses shot at. No guts, no guts . . . I wish they would let me have my way out here. There wouldn't be a gook or fucking reporter left in six months . . . our kids are dying out there right now while you guys are up here getting pissed . . . you're nothing but a bunch of yellow bastards."

He reminded me of that eccentric Englishman Lord Leconfield, who continued to ride to hounds during the Second World War, while most men of his class tried to give at least the appearance of austerity and sacrifice. One afternoon in 1940, in hot pursuit of the fox, he came upon a village soccer match. He reined in his horse and stood up in the stirrups fuming and shouted: "Haven't you people got anything better to do in wartime than play football?"

The memory of this bloodthirsty drunken Goldwater, this millionaire rag-trade merchant with White House pretensions and the man-

140

ners of a spoiled brat will always stay with me. A lot of revisionist drivel has been written about Goldwater in recent years. It is remarkable how easy it is for a man of Goldwater's limited talents to seduce the press and television into believing, or anyway reporting, that he is some kind of underappreciated sage of the West. It is inexplicable to me that Andy Rooney, among the most skeptical men I know, has fallen under this dull man's spell.

Patriotism is not, as Dr. Johnson said, the last refuge of the scoundrel. Folksiness is. The great reassessment of Goldwater occurred after his earthy call for Richard Nixon's resignation during Watergate. This was reported at the time as an act of great political courage, when in fact it was merely one opportunistic rat abandoning another who was drowning . . . even worse, he bit him as he was going down for the last time. There is, of course, never a last time for Richard Nixon. He has risen again, reducing old enemies like Goldwater to doddering members of the mouse pack.

I first met William F. Buckley in the Caravelle. It was in 1967 and he had stopped off in Saigon on his way to New Zealand. He called on me at the bureau.

"Mr. Safer," he said. "I'm Bill Buckley." Eyes flash, fangs glisten. "I've written some unkind things about you in my column. I thought I would come by and see what the monster looks like. A drink?"

I am sure many people find Buckley resistible. I am not among them. I think his geniality is genuine and his acid manner a bit of harmless shtick. He has tweaked me over the years, and I've tweaked him back. That afternoon in the bar of the Caravelle he was not the tendentious Buckley of *Firing Line* or the Neanderthal he sometimes appears to be in his column.

He had had his fill of official briefings and wanted to hear other voices, other views. Although he remained a true believer in the war, his columns were well layered with reasoned argument, not with the jingoism that some might have expected.

Buckley is the kind of polemicist who lives for the fight. I suspect that if the day dawned on the kind of Conservative Utopia he advocates he would bare his sword, or at least that viper's tongue, and work to destroy it.

There were other encounters in the Jerome et Juliet.

This was the place I first met Dan Rather. He had replaced me in London when I was sent to Vietnam at the beginning of 1965. At the end of the year he took over in Saigon, and I returned to the London bureau. In August 1966 we switched places once again. The day I arrived he introduced himself and invited me up to the bar for a drink. He could not have been more friendly.

A stream of admiration poured from his lips. A touch excessive, I thought, nevertheless very nice to hear. The man was trying very hard to be courtly, but the effect was destroyed by the strange way he was dressed. It was not the green army fatigues and combat boots—though it was most unusual for correspondents to be dressed for war in Saigon—it was the leather shoulder holster and nickel-plated Smith and Wesson .38 caliber revolver strapped on the outside of his clothing that gave an otherwise friendly encounter an edge of menace. I could not imagine who he might have to shoot in the Caravelle. The service was always quite good.

We chatted on about the war, New York, London. He told me how grateful he was for the hospitality my then girlfriend and I had shown Jean Rather back in London. There was a long silence, then he reached over and patted my arm and, unrelated to anything, said:

"*Nil carborundum,* Morley, *nil carborundum.*"

"What?"

"It's my favorite Latin phrase. It means, don't let the bastards get you down."

"Oh. I like *pax Britannica* a lot. *Ecce homo* is pretty good too."

"Yeah."

Dan has no recollection of the conversation and maintains that he never carried a gun in Vietnam or anywhere else. But "Don't let the bastards get you down" are good words to live by. Especially in this age, when humorless functionaries seem to have inherited the earth. *Nil carborundum,* Dan. *Gratia.* Thanks.

19

"The Best of the Best"

Ho Chi Minh City, January 25, 4:30 A.M.: I am up and out before dawn on this, my last full day in Vietnam. Tomorrow, Thursday evening, I must leave for Bangkok. I turn right and right again out of the Majestic, walking along the river front. I am determined to get lost, alone in the city. A television crew, no matter how convivial, is a kind of corporate caravan plodding noisily through peoples' lives, creating the illusion that the correspondent *is* alone, that each experience, each interview, and each encounter are fateful happenings on a random journey taken by this single traveler.

It is important to me to live the illusion, even for only a few hours. Perhaps ten blocks from the Majestic, slightly south and west of the hotel, I find what I am looking for. I am utterly lost in a warren of alleys intersected from time to time by broader avenues. I take a right turn into one of them keeping to the center of the empty roadway. Except for the odd cyclo, there is no traffic. The only light is from an occasional naked bulb. The only sound is a faint sighing and rustling of cloth. I begin to feel insecure . . . not the fear that could

144

suddenly seize me in some similar situation during the war, but something elemental, a gradual rising of panic in the chest. I imagine I see movement on the grass verge that separates the pavement from the sidewalk. It is not a single movement here and there, but an undulating wave that rises and settles on both sides of the street, sighing and rustling.

I feel surrounded by some awful presence. I reach into my shirt pocket for cigarettes and lighter. The pack comes out soaking wet. I am drenched with sweat in this cool morning air. Frightened sick, the way a child might feel alone in a forest full of phantoms. The sky lightens in a false dawn, and my phantoms are revealed: Ho Chi Minh City's homeless. Hundreds on this street alone. Here and there they are beginning to waken and rise from straw mats. There is an orderly quality, the way they have arranged themselves in perfect rows on either side of the street, as in some outdoor dormitory or military barracks. Some begin rolling their mats, organizing themselves for the day. Here and there men are wearing faded green South Vietnamese Army tunics, pulling on weather-beaten combat boots. A man approaches, uttering a mixture of English and Vietnamese that I cannot comprehend. I brush past him, fearful that offering a single cigarette might produce a riot. I hate myself for this arrogant crudeness, but not enough to stop and listen to him.

A block or so farther on, the street stalls are beginning to open. I stop at one and ask for coffee. A young woman nods, leaves, and returns with a steaming bowl of *soupe Chinois* and a baguette, the small French bread. The city is coming alive, beginning to swirl around me. The Saigonese, or whatever a native of Ho Chi Minh City is now called, pay little heed to the pale stranger on his stool. They are an independent-minded bunch . . . as curious as any people anywhere but too cool to show it. It is coming up to six-thirty in the morning, and I have promised to meet the caravan for break- fast at seven. I have had my brief hour of aloneness, lived the illu- sion we try so hard to create, got lost and frightened and even well fed.

145

The trouble is, I *really am* lost. I make for what I think is the general direction of the Majestic.

I continue to plod through alleys and eventually come out on a street lined on both sides by small soup stalls and curbside grocers. I scan faces, looking for someone of an age who might speak English or French. A haggard-looking man who has given up trying to get an ancient Solex moped started stares back at me.

"Can I help you?" he asks in almost perfect English.

"I'm lost; I'm trying to find my way to the old Majestic Hotel."

"If you call it the Majestic, this cannot be your first time in Vietnam. It is now the Cuu Long. Come, I will walk with you a part of the way."

"Where did you learn your excellent English?" I ask.

We walk on but he does not answer. The question, or perhaps the answer, is clearly troubling him. We continue for five minutes in silence. Finally he asks: "What are you doing here?" I explain the purpose of my journey, explain my earlier encounters with Vietnam.

"Will you have a cup of coffee?" he asks.

We stop at a stall and sip coffee, and he introduces himself. "My name is Pham Van Thuong. But please call me Frank. That's what they called me in Mike force."

The Mike forces were mercenary troops, mainly Cambodian, Montagnard, and Nung tribesmen and some Vietnamese, who were commanded by twelve-man teams of American Special Forces. They were officially known as Mobile Strike Forces, reduced to "Mike" as in the military radio designation for M.

They were among the best-trained and most reliable troops in South Vietnam, partly because they were well fed, well led, and well paid. They were also among the most cruel. In a Mike force barracks near Ben Cat, I saw a dozen mason jars filled with ears that Nung mercenaries had cut from the bodies of their victims. The so-called ethnic minorities in Vietnam, like the Nungs and Montagnards, have a finely tuned hatred for all Vietnamese. Joe Stringham, a Special Forces captain and the bravest man I knew in Vietnam, once walked

146

the gauntlet between two companies of his Mike force at Ben Cat, bent on killing each other. The Nungs were on one side of the camp, the Vietnamese on the other. Both sides were firing automatic weapons, and the Nungs had already killed four Vietnamese troopers.

Stringham walked between them firing his Colt .45 service automatic in the air, shouting, "Ngung! Thoi! Stop! Enough!"

Joe Stringham, now in his fifties, a colonel who still jumps out of airplanes, had all the qualities that should have brought him to the highest positions of command. It was those very qualities, of course, that stunted his career—gallantry, an inability to lie to either his men or his superiors, and patriotism that was founded on compassion, not bravado. For such a man there is little room at the top.

After the war, members of Mike force, especially the Vietnamese, were sought by the victors with special zeal.

Sitting on the stools, sipping coffee, Frank tells me: "I was near Danang, but when things began to collapse I came back to Saigon to see if my wife was all right. I had been trying to make some contact with my American friends . . . I knew so many of them . . . I had been in Mike force from almost the beginning. I was the interpreter for so many different Americans. The radio man and the interpreter. But when I got here they had all gone. I tried to get to the embassy, but it was impossible. I guess I looked to everyone like another ARVN soldier who just deserted. I was not . . . I think I was special. All those years in Mike force and still alive . . . I think that is some kind of record.

"It's funny, you know, the Americans always called us 'The Best of the Best,' . . . then they left.

"They came for me . . . the VC came for me just days after Saigon fell. I think I was denounced by a friend. I knew they were looking for anyone who had any connection with the Americans, and Mike force had a bad reputation. They questioned me for a few months . . . that's when I lost most of my teeth; then they sent me for reeducation to a camp in Tay Ninh Province."

147

"Did you get reeducated?"

"Ha . . . it was a kind of show. They would give us lectures, and then we were made to stand up and confess our sins and apologize. We all had to sign a paper that we had committed atrocities. No one believed the lectures; no one believed the confessions. We were all like actors. Reeducation was mostly hard labor . . . hard labor for ten years."

"Ten years?"

"Yeah . . . the ARVN guys, the officers were in for five or six . . . they saved the worst punishment for the best of the best."

"Did your wife visit you?"

"Once. At Tet, I forget what year it was, maybe 1978 . . . I told her not to come back. She had a job with the committee for Ho Chi Minh City in the foreign department because she can speak and type English and French. It was too dangerous for her to admit openly that I was in reeducation camp."

We are the subject of some curiosity in the street . . . not me so much . . . but who is this Vietnamese who is chatting so cozily in English?

"Aren't you concerned about sitting here talking to me?" I ask.

"What can they do to us? . . . The day I came back from the camp they fired my wife from her job with the city. They told her they did not want the wife of a criminal working with them. They won't let us work, and they won't let us leave."

"Honestly, how bad were you guys in the Mike force . . . we heard a lot of stories."

"Bad things happened. Everybody has a story he would rather not tell. I forget how it started, the business of the ears . . . I don't remember if the VC did it first or if we did it first. The Nungs were the worst . . . you could say they were the worst of the best."

"And you?"

"I was a radio operator . . . I stayed with my captain, my American. He did not want to know. I did not want to know."

148

I tell him I must leave. I must not be late at the Majestic for what will be my third breakfast of the day.

"Please, won't you come around the corner? I would like you to meet Jeannette, my wife . . . she runs a rattan shop . . . she was able to get the license."

"I cannot . . . I am late. I promise I will be back tomorrow."

He pleads with me.

"I promise," I tell him. "I will come back."

Flashbacks

20

The Pain that Lingers

7:30 A.M.: The caravan is waiting at the Majestic. Miss Mai is looking very smug. She's been wedding shopping in Ho Chi Minh City, which for someone from Hanoi is the equivalent of Hong Kong or Bangkok. She is due to be married in a few weeks to a young Hanoi diplomat. Although she is pleased about all the goodies she's found . . . raw silk for a wedding dress, boxes of sweets, and small gifts for relatives . . . I am not so sure she is so sure about the groom. When he receives his first diplomatic posting, she will not be allowed to travel with him. Without a great deal of confidence, she'd already told me "the reason for this is that we are a poor country, and we cannot afford to send a whole family overseas."

I suspect there are other reasons, other concerns. The success of overseas Vietnamese is known to everyone here. Hanoi will not allow its most talented young people to witness the prosperity of their cousins and perhaps be tempted away from duty to the motherland.

Morley Safer

We are due to leave for a drive to Cu Chi. In the hotel lobby I tell Miss Mai I have a favor to ask.

"What is it?" she asks.

"I have an old friend in Ho Chi Minh City whom I have not seen for almost twenty years. Could you arrange for me to meet him tonight."

I write the name Pham Xuan An on a piece of paper. It means nothing to her. She summons an assistant minder, a young, well-meaning, but barely competent boy named Tuan. He looks at the name and goes ice cold.

"I will make inquiries," he says. "I will let you know this evening."

The question of asking to see An has been troubling me for weeks. Back in New York I was tempted to include a request to see him on the official list that the Vietnamese wanted from us before the visas were granted. I decided against it in the belief that it would make the government suspicious of our purpose in Vietnam. At dinner in Bangkok the night before I flew to Hanoi, journalist and author David Butler had asked if I was going to see An to clear up a mystery that has been hanging over the name since the fall of Saigon, fourteen years ago.

"Maybe," I said.

Pham Xuan An was a correspondent for *Time* magazine in Saigon. His beat was Vietnamese politics and military affairs. He was among the best connected journalists in the country. At *Time* he was considered a sage. It was always An who would brief new correspondents; it was An who even the competition sought when trying to unravel the hopelessly complicated threads of Vietnamese political loyalties.

An was an open and engaging man with a wonderful sense of humor, always welcome at American and Vietnamese military and diplomatic occasions, one of the few Vietnamese reporters admitted to off-the-record briefings by the American mission. It was rumored that he was a CIA agent.

It is known that during the last days of Saigon An had persuaded

151

American officials to take a number of Vietnamese friends out of the country . . . people who would have certainly been on the Communist list of public enemies. On the very last day he managed to get his wife and two small children onto a plane. He, too, was cleared to leave, but he missed the flight.

There were rumors that he was dead . . . that he had been arrested and was still rotting in a reeducation camp . . . that he was a full colonel in the People's Army.

As young Tuan leaves with my piece of paper, I have little hope that anything will come of this request.

There is a dreamlike quality to the drive to Cu Chi. It is only twenty-five miles northwest of Ho Chi Minh City, but the trip sets up in the brain a confusion of realities. I have been there a dozen times or more, but only once by road. The helicopter is a fine way to travel, but it induces a view of the world that only God and CEOs share on a regular basis. The big picture takes on a hypnotic clarity, skipping over the peskier small realities of the earthbound. In New York the titans of industry and commerce commute to their weekend dachas in the Hamptons by helicopter, accompanied often by editors and publishers and so-called opinion makers. The opinions that are made reflect each other's needs. The mogul gets his celebrity-approval and possibly a free ride in the financial columns . . . the hitchhiker gets his free ride, avoiding the boiling hell of the Long Island Expressway. Together, five thousand feet above it, the two agree that the big picture looks pretty good.

Is that what happened here? The shamelessly prodigal generals who ran this war literally skipped over the hot, hard parts of the place in cool isolation. From the air, from a two-star general's altitude, the landscape always looks pacified. His helicopter rarely hits potholes.

The road to Cu Chi, if you stay with it long enough, will take you all the way to Phnom Penh. It passes through some of the richest land in Vietnam and through the spiritual heart of the movement that became known as the Vietcong. Saigon intellectuals and distant

152

Hanoi ideologues may have directed the movement, but here, in the agricultural suburbs of the capital, passions were stirred that went beyond ideology. During the most repressive years of Diem and his successors, these people lived under their own shadow government, functioned with their own schools and self-help organizations, were merciless in dealing with traitors, and showed the most extraordinary courage in battle. This is the lower end of what became known as the Iron Triangle, one minute from Saigon by fighter-bomber, seconds away from the artillery firebases that surrounded it.

There is an allegorical quality about the war that was fought here. While Frank Borman was walking on the moon, we were turning the paddy land and eucalyptus forests and rubber plantations of Binh Duong and Hau Nghia Province into a moonscape. The people endured in relocation camps we created or underground in stinking infested tunnels that all our courage and determination and sophisticated gases could not eliminate. If the war could not be won in the Iron Triangle, then the war could not be won. It was a triumph of the will, of ingenuity and primitivism over the juggernauts of science and industry.

Today on either side of the road to Cu Chi I am witnessing the happy destruction of the very thing these people, unwittingly or not, tried so hard to create. They call this battle *doi moi,* renovation, the dismantling of the crackpot economic system imposed by the geriatric theorists in Hanoi.

Businesses of every kind are flourishing. I am told that when the Sixth Party Congress gave its approval to privatization in 1986 the first business to open printed business cards. The owner knew what he was doing. He was swamped with orders as the word spread. Entrepreneurship meant an identity. An address had a meaning; work had a purpose beyond mere subsistence.

I cannot believe the life that is now swelling up from the wasteland that surrounded Cu Chi. There are weavers and dyers, furniture makers and smithies. Here more than anywhere I have the feeling

153

that Vietnam will be the next pool of cheap labor in the West's insatiable demand for disposable durables. For the moment it has the idyllic feeling of a country market . . . flax drying in the sun, great bolts of red and orange linen stretched over their drying racks. The rich colors and the harsh morning sun make the roadside seem ablaze in a benign Technicolor fire storm. Behind the stalls the jungle and the paddies have reclaimed their rights. Once again it strikes me . . . no evidence. We were never here. The conflicting realities of what was and what is.

I am in Cu Chi to talk to Van Le, a veteran of the fighting in the Iron Triangle. We meet in a small glade of eucalyptus, just beyond the town. There is a soda-pop stand tended by a granny and behind it a thatched house with pigs and chickens making an absolute hash of the garden. The day and the scene have an almost literary perfection about them. Someone is needed to articulate the relationship between men and women and land, and of course the heat. It is Faulkner country this morning.

It is cooler among the eucalyptus, with just enough breeze to make the leaves rustle . . . turning gray green to silver as they catch the light.

Van Le is a slim man with a thatch of unruly black hair. He is wearing a starched blue shirt, the color of the sky, dark trousers, and flip-flops. He has the smooth skin of a child, but his eyes have such intensity it is difficult to maintain contact. His eyes seem filled with black fire.

He is a Northerner, from Than Hoa Province south of Hanoi. In 1965 his entire Young Communist Youth Group volunteered for the army.

"My father was very proud," he tells me. "My father was an active revolutionary. He was so pleased that his eldest son would go to the front . . . that I would be an example for others who might want to shirk their duty."

He was sixteen years old.

154

In 1966, after six months of basic training, he walked South, first to a base in Kontum Province, then to Tay Ninh to a big base camp that was a joint North Vietnamese-Vietcong staging area. He was sent from there to the northern Cu Chi District.

"We lived like rats," he says. "In the tunnels day and night. It seemed like the bombing never stopped . . . if I tried to go outside there was napalm and antipersonnel bombs . . . if I stayed inside they used the big bombs, the ones that go deep underground and then explode. That was the worst fear . . . of the tunnels collapsing, of dying like a rat.

"The biggest day of my life at age nineteen was the day I walked into a village with some civilians, and we went to a market and bought tea and ate some sweets. You cannot imagine what it was like to breathe real air and to have the sunshine on your face.

"It was September in 1967. It was the next day that became the worst day of my life."

His boyish, calm face with those blazing eyes is starting to come apart. Miss Mai, whose translation so far has been coldly professional, unemotional in its delivery, is clearly affected. Her voice rises . . . those etched-in-steel features are softening.

Van Le continues: "The next morning, very early in the morning, the artillery started. It was from the guns of the American 25th Division.

"Then we heard the helicopters coming; they seemed to be coming from every direction, and they dropped the troops off in some deserted fields. They came toward the village, but when we started firing they withdrew, and afterward the Americans started to shell us with the special colored smoke bombs to mark our positions. I was very frightened because the smoke was coming very close. When the artillery started again, one of the first shells fell fifty meters away, and two of my comrades, in the very next bunker, were killed.

"The Americans started coming again, but they were behind a green fence, and we couldn't see them well."

155

"You mean the tree line?" I ask.

"Yes. They were protected by the trees, and then they started to spread out. In the bunker I told one of the soldiers—there were three of us in the bunker—I told him to go out and see what the Americans were going to do. But he refused to go. He was a new drafted soldier, and it was his first battle, and he just lay on the ground shaking. I had to go. I was the leader. The nineteen-year-old leader.

"When I came out of the bunker, I saw a big American creeping toward our shelter. He was facedown in the underbrush, and I think he was trying to get behind a tree. All I could see were his shoulders and his helmet, a green helmet . . . and I still remember the sight . . . I remember that it looked like a big beetle coming toward me, coming right at me!"

The words are rushing out of his mouth. He pauses. His face is contorted, and he is swallowing hard, trying to hold back not only the tears that finally spring to those black eyes, but the filmstrip of memory that is so plainly racing through his mind.

Miss Mai too is swallowing hard. She is no longer the bossy bureaucrat, dutifully translating heroic war stories for the government. She is a kid witnessing, perhaps for the first time, genuine grief. I look away from Van Le's face; it is bent to one side, his eyes focused past me. Again, the thousand-yard stare of boys who aged overnight. His body quivers in a deep sigh, and he goes on:

"He kept coming toward me, and I knew if he saw me he would kill me. There were only fifty meters between us. I raised my rifle and started to shoot. One. Two. Three shots. I saw the helmet jump up a little, and then it laid still. The beetle laid still.

"I was not sure he was dead. I waited until four o'clock, after all the Americans had left, and then I scrambled toward the tree, and he was there a few meters from the tree. He was dead . . . I think he died immediately from the first shot. I took his watch, and I took his M-16, and I took some pictures he had in his wallet . . . they were pictures of him and a woman and two small children. He was a black man."

156

"How did you feel . . . I mean about killing another man?"

"At the time I felt nothing. After the peace I went back to the North to my home village, and I saw those mothers of friends of mine who had been killed in the war. In the group of twenty boys who joined the army, only ten of us came back. I saw how much those mothers suffered. I thought of the American mothers.

"I think any bullet, from whoever it comes, is shot at the mother first, not at the son who is killed."

"Do you think about the American you killed?"

"It started in 1980. I began to feel a terrible sadness. I began to think of the past, and I find I think of it every day. I do not have nightmares. I think it is a gift to me from God that I do not have nightmares. But in the day I think about it; I think about the war every day. I have three sons now. I would *never, never* send them off to war."

His words have a chilling echo. Only weeks ago in New York Diane Evans, a Vietnam veteran, an American Army nurse, told me: "You know, I think about it every day . . . I think about Vietnam every day."

Van Le has pulled himself together. There is a long pause, when I ask him if he knew the name of the American he killed.

"I knew it but I've forgotten. I turned in all the documents I took from him to my commander. But I kept one photograph for a while. It was evidence that I killed an American. I lost it during the Tet battle. Now when I tell you this story from my past about the time I killed another person, I do not get any pleasure. I don't like the idea of having to tell this story to anyone. I think I've only told it once before, to a close friend."

This business of the photographs devastates me. Weeks ago, going through old notebooks, I found four postage-stamp-sized pictures and a larger snapshot of a young man being directed by an older man in the use of an assault rifle. The four miniatures were of Marx, Lenin, Engels, and Ho Chi Minh. The pictures had been taken from a prisoner or a corpse by an American adviser some-

157

where south of Can Tho. Both sides took and kept each other's snapshots. There must be something primeval about it. Taking an enemy's strength, taking his luck. I must burn those photographs when I get home or send them anonymously back to Vietnam. The thought that I kept these pitiful souvenirs, these saints some young man carried into battle, makes me feel unclean. I silently apologize to Van Le.

The interview is over. Before we return to Ho Chi Minh City, we go for a short walk through the eucalyptus. Van Le tells me he chose to stay on in the South, where he finds it easier to work.

He feels lucky, he says. "So many of the veterans came back to what they thought would be a normal life, but they couldn't even find a job."

Van Le is working for the United Film Studio in Ho Chi Minh City, writing screenplays. He's also written short stories and a few novels. All of them are about the war. As we leave he gives us a poem he'd just completed, a poem about American GIs who've returned to Vietnam:

> There's an American soldier
> Who returns to northern Cu Chi.
> He bends his back to the tunnels.
> What does he see? What does he think?
>
> There's a Vietnamese hero
> Now a grandfather.
> He asks the American to share wine
> Outside the tunnel.
>
> Each man is silent
> As he looks into the other's eyes.
> Something is rising like a deep pain.
>
> The war was terrible
> All that time past.
> The dead lost their bodies.
> The living lost their homes.

Morley Safer

How many American soldiers
Died in this land?
How many Vietnamese
Lie buried under trees and grass?

The pain still lingers.
Why should we remember it?
We are old, our era past.
Our mistakes belong to bygone days.

Now the wineglass joins friends in peace.
The old men lift their glasses.
Tears run down their cheeks.

He recites it for the camera, rushing through it, it seems, to avoid breaking down again. The words are barked out, almost in anger. When he is finished he is exhausted. His body sags, but the black eyes continue to blaze.

I can imagine that zealous sixteen-year-old, shouting the approved slogans, his youth movement bandana neatly in place, the eyes on fire as he marches off to kill the imperialists. He found one and killed one and killed something of himself as well.

159

21

Hapless Heroes

2:00 P.M.: At the Majestic a man is waiting for me. He offers his card. It says he is chief of the press bureau, Office of External Relations.

"There are two men who have asked to see you," he says. "They have a letter for you. You don't have to talk to them if you don't want to. They want money. If you want, I will get rid of them."

Over his shoulder I see two Vietnamese men in their fifties. They are both extremely nervous. They look as if they are on a mission of great danger, that the mere act of dealing with an official of the city administration and asking to see a foreigner and coming to the Majestic involved great risk and greater courage.

The letter is addressed to MR. GENERAL MANAGER, CBS MAIN OFFICE, NEW YORK. It begins:

"More than thirteen years ago after the fall of Saigon (30 April 1975) we, DUONG-THE-TU, alias LE-VIET, reporter, and TRAN-DUC-SUU, cameraman, had worked full time for CBS Saigon Bureau from 1

May 1975 to 31 May 1975. But since then we two persons had not got pay yet. The reason why it happened so complicatedly and haplessly is as follows."

Complicatedly and haplessly. In three words these two unfortunate men had written a complete history of the war. The letter goes on to describe their employment by CBS News the day after the fall; how they had worked for a month filing stories to New York; how they, with others, had been "nominated as CBS heros at the time"; and how, thirty days after their employment, all communications had ended except for a cable from New York saying it was forbidden by U.S. law to send them dollars, but their salaries would be banked in a "big American Bank for security and benefits."

The sums involved are pitifully small . . . together they equal about two hours' work for one of the three network anchormen . . . around three thousand dollars.

The letter ends: "Now we run short of money and have to live a hard life as you should know our situation. Would you please, being on the humanitarian act of the American Custom, pay our salaries . . . as wrote in the Petty Cash Vouchers.

"We are longing for your humanitarian reply, meanwhile, we remain Dear Sir, Respectfully yours."

I approach the two men, who are squatting deferentially in front of the gentleman from External Relations. They are practically quivering with fear.

"I will see that your letter gets to the right people," I tell them. Their eyes dart to Mr. External Relations. I walk them to the other side of the lobby with the excuse that I must be nearer to the light to take their pictures so that New York will know their stories are genuine.

"Please, dear sir, Mr. Morley, we are desperate for the money," Suu says. "Please ask . . ." and he reels off a string of familiar names, American and Vietnamese, people he knew had been evacuated to New York and Washington during the last chaotic days of Saigon.

161

"Do not worry. I will see that you and Mr. Tu get your money . . . by the way, how did you know I was here in Ho Chi Minh City?"

Suu laughs out loud, ". . . it is still Saigon, Mr. Morley . . . everyone knows everything . . . and if they do not, then they make up a story. A taxi driver saw you the day you arrived at Tan Son Nhut."

I take their pictures and their letter and promise once again to send them to the CBS accounting people. Will a molasses-paced corporate giant understand the urgency of Suu's situation? I fear that his long-ing for a humanitarian reply will go unheeded. Not even he, after fourteen years of waiting, understands the gap between the fleeting good intentions of those who send people to gather news and the bean counters who reluctantly pay the bills. It has always been this way. In the heat of the moment the story is the thing and seems worth getting for any promise, any price. The cables of congratula-tions go out, all the heartfelt but cheap-at-the-price sentiments are expressed. In days the story gives way to other stories, other prom-ises, other cables. It has always been this way, but now it is worse. The newsrooms are still run with the same dedication by men of talent and sensitivity. But the newsrooms are owned by complex institutions blinded by profit. News is not sacred, but it is also not a commodity. It has become one, interchangeable with game shows. The pressures put on the president of a news division to keep the commodity price up force him to pitch it in the manner of a super-market comic strip, "inquiring minds want to know . . . ," tinker with it, re-create it when necessary, and possibly lose it entirely behind the foggy screen of "infotainment." The news joins refrigerators, mi-crowaves, jet engines, and the flogging of hotel rooms, as a product.

There used to be a clearly defined ethos in each of the networks. The ethos today is as permanent as an arbitrageur's smile. Today the bean counters wear their titles with jauntiness and pride. The new true lords of journalism.

Mr. Suu and Mr. Tu solemnly shake my hand. Each is carrying in

162

his other hand a clutch of battered gray CBS News interoffice pouches, filled with petty-cash slips, promissory notes a generation old. They hold on to these disintegrating gray envelopes as if they held some yet-to-be-revealed divine truth. Passports to a new Jerusalem.

As the two are ushered out the door of the Majestic by Mr. External Affairs' flapping hands, Suu shouts over his shoulder: "When CBS opens another Saigon bureau once again in the future, Mr. Morley, please you have two good local men."

Mr. External Affairs stands with his hands folded across his chest on the Majestic's steps and watches them disappear in the crowd along Bach Dang Boulevard. He has his little triumph for the day.*

I excuse myself and tell him I am going for a walk. I've been told to take a look at the Brink Hotel.

The Brink is one of Saigon's few tall buildings, an ugly concrete affair built along the lines of a London "tower block," a public housing project. It is the kind of construction in which no economy has been spared, no mistake corrected. Placed as it is, near the Continental Palace Hotel and the Opera House, it has the look of an uninvited bumpkin at a dowager's tea party. After the Paris peace talks the Brink housed embassy staff and officials of the U.S. Defense Attaché's Office. Before the withdrawal of American forces, it was one of the largest officers' billets in Vietnam. It had a rooftop restaurant whose GI chefs boasted they served the best steaks in town. They were, until they got into the hands of the GI chefs, who must have believed that "rare" or even "medium rare" represented communist sympathies. The favored food color was gray.

---

*On returning from Vietnam at the end of January 1989, I passed Mr. Suu's and Mr. Tu's claim to the CBS accounting department, which on checking its files, conceded that the debt was outstanding and would be paid immediately. In July I received a letter from the two men, written in the same tortured ornate style, saying they were still "awaiting the fulfillment of the CBS obligation" but that they were confident that "the humanitarian justice of CBS" would soon prevail. In October 1989 I was assured by a CBS vice president that the debt was paid in full.

163

The restaurant seemed to live independently of Vietnam, of the war, of any of the realities of the world below. It was kept at an arctic temperature, with music that ran the gamut from Tony Bennett to Dean Martin. It was a hollow version of an American suburban restaurant populated mainly by Saigon warriors. There were colonels from logistics and supply, paymasters, and hundreds of planners: first lieutenant planners right up to brigadier general planners. A lament, popular among GIs and written by an anonymous grunt, went:

'Scuse me General Westy, I hate to bother you,
But I've got a couple of problems,
And I don't know what to do.
My air conditioner's broke,
My sedan's outa gas,
Besides all this, well, I can't get a seven-day pass.

I'm a Saigon Warrior, I'm helping fight a war.
Pushin' a pencil, my finger's getting sore.

Well now, since I've been "In-Country"—that's military
for "here"—I've learned to speak the language,
I'm winning hearts and minds.

I can say fluently . . . "Tudo," "Saigon Tea," . . . "I love you
too much," "massage?" "Hey, where you go now?"
"Money changed?"
        "dee-dee . . . you buy for me . . ."

I'm a Saigon Warrior, I'm helping fight a war.
Pushin' a pencil, my finger's getting sore.

In the field line officers referred to them as REMFs—rear-echelon mother-fuckers. Indeed the Brink knew no war was going on, not until Christmas Eve 1964.

Two Vietcong guerrillas, dressed as South Vietnamese soldiers, parked a car loaded with plastic explosive in front of the hotel. It blew up at the cocktail hour, killing two Americans and wounding fifty-eight.

164

Morley Safer

In front of the Brink today stands a free-form wall. At its center in bas-relief is a depiction of dead and dying Americans, with the words:

> At three minutes to six on 24.12.64, two of our Sapper Units bravely and cleverly using an American sedan containing two hundred kilograms of dynamite blew up the inside of the Brink officers' project killing and wounding 142 Americans and destroying 24 army trucks and their communications network.

The sight of the dead men so carefully engraved in the stone and the inflated claims make me feel slightly sick. Praising their heroes was enough. It makes the point. The local minder who translates the inscription seems utterly oblivious to both the words and the stone scene of carnage. He feels neither pride nor shame. He is only a boy, to whom this building is nothing more than another faceless ministry. The historic marker could be celebrating an event as distant as the martyrdom of the Trung sisters.

News, I decide, is farce, especially old, tragic news. "The Brink"— it could have been the name of an English country house in a play by Richard Brinsley Sheridan or Oscar Wilde. In fact, it was named after Brigadier General Francis G. Brink, the very first American commander in Vietnam who, shortly after returning to Washington in the 1950s, closed the door of his Pentagon office one morning and quietly blew his brains out.

22

My Fair Lady

4:00 P.M.: Her name is Tran Thi Gung. She is forty-two, and among the many medals she has been awarded is one honoring her as a Hero American Killer.

She lives with her husband and three children at 164B Tran Hung Dao Street. To get to her second-floor flat, you must walk through a tailor and dressmaking shop, which for reasons I cannot recall now, only hours later as I write up my notes, I have called "Rosie's."

Walking through Rosie's with the full caravan plus cameras and lights, past customers, fitters, and seamstresses, we are barely noticed. This quality of the Vietnamese, or at least the Saigonese, to withhold curiosity is mystifying. Elsewhere the presence of television paraphernalia invites choruses of questions, requests to "take my picture," demands for written authority to photograph. Here, not even a curious glance. Almost as if they were actors on a sound stage, preparing to go through their assigned roles, ordered to be heedless of the technology recording them.

166

On the second-floor landing is the kitchen where Gung is shredding an old copy of *Nhan Dan,* the party newspaper. She puts a match to the paper and stuffs it, along with some wood scraps, into a small stove and sets a pot of rice on the grate.

She is a small sinewy woman with lively dark eyes. She is still quite attractive, but when she smiles the corners of her mouth twist downward, giving her face a cast of cruelty.

When we talk about the war she is so completely matter-of-fact as to give a hint of arrogance. It is not arrogance, I decide, but a pushy, city-kid toughness, the kind you find among young women in Brooklyn or in the East End of London.

The pot of rice is beginning to simmer now, and she gives it a nudge with her bare hand to stop it from going on the boil . . . narrow delicate hands, but with palms as hard as a blacksmith's. The pot contains the evening meal for her family; her youngest, a ten-year-old boy, has not yet come home from school. She wonders where he can be; he should have been home half an hour ago.

She says her father was killed by the puppet army in 1964, and shortly after, friends of his came to the house and told her she should take up the fight. She was sixteen when she joined the movement. She was the fourth of five children. An older brother was already a Vietcong soldier. She does not talk about the other three.

She spent most of the war in the Cu Chi District . . . almost all of the fighting was with Americans of the 25th Infantry Division based at Dong Zu. Her tunnel complex was less than a kilometer away from the base perimeter.

"From that close it was easy to watch their movements. They were very careless. We always knew exactly when they were going to attack. We would not fire until they were less than twenty meters away."

"Did you kill many Americans?"

She lets out a laugh. "Yes, many." She is totally oblivious to any feelings I may have . . . or to the current party line of reconciliation.

167

Miss Mai simply shrugs and translates. Gung is incapable of being lectured. It would be like telling a piranha to please act like a golden retriever in front of the guests.

Plain talk is what she gives and what she expects. A Vietnamese Eliza Doolittle, I decide. She once helped her mother run a vegetable and flower stall at the Saigon central market. Eliza Doolittle with a war for a Professor Higgins who helped her discover that she was extremely adept at killing people.

"You killed a lot of people . . . do you have any regrets now, ten, fifteen years later?"

"No."

"None?"

"No. If I had not shot them, they would have killed me."

"Any thoughts about their mothers or their wives; any bad dreams?"

"No. I sometimes dream about the fighting, but I would not call them bad dreams. If I were to think about mothers and wives, I would think about the Vietnamese mothers and wives. The Americans should have stayed home."

"Have you ever met an American, talked to one?"

"Yes. I captured one. They gave me a medal for it."

I ask for details.

"There were three of us, me and two men. We had orders to set up a road block on the highway coming out of Cu Chi. We would collect a road tax sometimes that way. A military truck came along, and it wouldn't stop, so we shot out the tires, and it went into the ditch. We captured three of them. Two puppet soldiers and this big American.

"We took their weapons . . . but we could not take the rice, so we burned it and set fire to the truck. My two comrades took the Vietnamese away. They told me to take the American back to our commander."

"What happened to the Vietnamese?"

"I don't know."

"What did you do with the American?"

"I told him to take off his shoes and throw them away. I was afraid he would try to run away. I had my rifle and his M-16 and his leather bag . . . he had this leather bag, and it was full of money. Thousands of Vietnamese piasters and a lot of the American military money."

The American military money was called MPC—military payment certificate. In mid-1965 the Saigon command banned the use of dollars by American army personnel. GIs were playing the black market with dollars, and it was having a ruinous effect on an already ruined economy. They replaced the dollars with military scrip, which of course immediately found its own price level on the Chinese-operated Saigon black market. With the truckload of rice and the piasters, her captive most likely was an American adviser to an ARVN unit . . . or conceivably, someone running his own little business on the side. It was not unheard of.

"He was very frightened," she says. "He said 'If you are going to shoot me, let me know several minutes ahead of time, so I can prepare for my death . . . please tell me now, before you tie my eyes up.' He was very frightened, but in a way he was very brave too. I told him now we would have to feed him, not shoot him. I was going to take him to my base . . . and I cannot tie your eyes; if I did, you would not be able to see to walk to the base.

"On the way we walked through a hamlet, and there were some women there, and they ran and got sticks and tried to beat him. I told them to stop. He was my responsibility, and I had orders to take him to the base commander. They must have been mothers of guerrillas.

"He started to complain that his feet were hurting, but I told him to keep walking. I think the Americans aren't used to walking barefoot the way we are.

"He spoke to me in Vietnamese. He said he had studied it for six months in the United States. He told me he wanted to give me his watch. I told him I don't need a watch . . . I already have a watch. He then offered me his pen. I already had a pen, so I said no. He

169

told me he was twenty and asked me how old I was, and I told him I was nineteen.

"I made him walk ahead of me by some distance because I was afraid he would try to take the guns away from me if he was too close. He was so big, and I am so small. This man was the first American I had ever seen up close. I had been told the Americans were very ugly, but this man was tall with fair hair and very light skin, and he was very handsome."

The room collapses in laughter when she points to the cameraman, Wade Bingham, and says: "He was as tall as him, but much, much thinner, and he had hair on his head.

"As we came near the base he told me I was pretty, and again he offered me his watch and his pen. Again I said no. If I took his presents, I might feel that I had to release him. I suppose he was hoping for something like that."

"Tell me, Gung . . . if the circumstances had been different . . . if there wasn't a war, do you think the story might have had a different ending . . . you and your American prisoner?"

Something approaching a blush crosses her face, and she looks up to the landing where her husband is watching. She gives a broad smile and a "what-the-hell-who-knows?" shrug of her shoulders.

"What happened to him when you got him to the base?"

"My friends were furious with me. They asked: 'Why did you not blindfold him . . . you have orders to blindfold prisoners?' It is stupid, I told them. How could he walk blindfolded . . . and anyway he was too tall for me to blindfold. He would have overpowered me and probably killed me. Then they asked him a lot of questions, intelligence information. I don't remember what he answered."

"And then?"

"I don't know."

"Did they kill him?"

"This was not the policy. I suppose they sent him North and he was exchanged."

170

Morley Safer

I believe her. Or I believe she believes it to be the truth. I do not think Eliza Doolittle-Gung is capable of saying anything but what she really thinks.

She leaves the pot to simmer, and we walk up the half-dozen steps to the apartment's main room. It is a combination living-dining room and children's bedroom. Her husband is at the dining table reading his evening paper. Two daughters, fourteen and twelve, are squeezed into an easy chair whispering to each other. They have just returned from school and have that Vietnamese ability to look cool and fresh at the end of a long humid day. Both are very beautiful and, I decide, extremely pampered. Not by their mother.

At one end of the room are French windows that open onto a narrow balcony overlooking Tran Hung Dao Street. The effect is very Parisian. Trees, not the plane trees of Paris, but something much like them, do not really obstruct the view; they soften it. In the failing light the view is a nineteenth-century painting. Down below three road workers are hacking away at the pavement. There is a painting by Manet called *The Pavers of the Rue de Berne,* and except for the absence of horse and carriage, he might well have set his easel on this balcony.

The European spell is broken by the sounds and smells of an approaching Asian evening. The thick scent of durian and exhaust fumes and *nuoc mam* drifts up from the stalls. The click-clack of the soup sellers begins, accompanied by a coughing chorus of Japanese mopeds. The room is sparsely furnished. In the corner there are cots for the children. Against one wall is a dresser and next to it the dining table with a vase holding some paper flowers. They have the look of a school project. Against the other wall is an elaborate shrine with a faded photograph of a middle-aged man. In front of it are some pots holding wilting marigolds and on an altar a jar of burning joss sticks. Beneath the photograph are four smaller ones, of a young woman and three young men.

Gung introduces me to her husband, a man in his early fifties.

Flashbacks

They met in the jungle near Cu Chi. He is now a colonel in the traffic section of the Ho Chi Minh City police department.

I point to the large photograph.

"My father," he says. "He joined the revolution in 1945. He was arrested many times by the French. When I was growing up, he was hardly ever home. He spent most of the time in jail. They tortured him . . . and then came the turn of the puppets, and they tortured him too.

"There were ten of us, ten children, and all of us followed his example and joined the fight."

"How many came back?"

"I lost my three younger brothers. They were killed in the war. My sister . . . she died in prison. She was tortured over a long period by soldiers, Vietnamese soldiers, and she died of the torture. We never saw her body. My father died in 1969. I think he just gave up living. He was in his fifties, my age now."

"Do you hate the Americans now?"

"I hated them then, and I hate them now . . . and the French before them. Look what you did to our country. Before the war my family was quite well-to-do. We had a very nice house. Never mind the politics; all we believed in was our country, the right to have our own country . . . and you came here and tried to take that right away from us. When I came back from the war, after liberation, the house was gone, totally destroyed by your bombs."

Gung seems quite indifferent to the emotion being shown by her husband, as if she regards the war as a perfectly orderly act of nature that had to be dealt with, like flood or drought. He is still outraged.

The room falls silent as a boy of ten, smartly turned out in starched white shirt and blue shorts, comes running in, sobbing. His two sisters begin to giggle, begin to tease him, which of course only intensifies his sobs.

"Where have you been?" demands Gung.

Hiccuping through his choked throat, he explains that he was kept

172

late at school by a cruel and inhuman teacher who had falsely accused him of talking in class while her back was turned. He explains that he was not the culprit but that when the teacher demanded that he name the offender he refused, and he had to pay the penalty himself. Gung gives him an affectionate pat on the head and begins to set the table for dinner. Her husband lifts him up, and the boy embraces him, his face nuzzled into his father's neck. The boy's tears begin to stain the father's shirt.

On a ceiling beam is a framed piece of silk; pinned to it are seven medals, two on top and five underneath.

"Who do the medals belong to?"

"The two on top are mine," says Gung. "One, I was awarded for capturing the American . . . the other was just for fighting Americans. The five others belong to both of us. They give them for serving in the army . . . if you were in long enough, you get them. It's nothing. It's automatic."

"Do you have more?"

"Yes, somewhere." She opens the dresser drawer, rummages through spools of thread and half-darned socks. She pulls out a framed diploma with a medal attached to it, hands it to me without looking up. "Hero of the revolution," she mutters. And then:

"Here it is . . . this is what you want to see."

She hands me a piece of gold-colored metal attached to a piece of red-and-yellow silk.

"Hero American killer."

Her black eyes are dancing; she is smiling that down-in-the-corners smile.

In my hand the cheap alloy medal is almost weightless.

Flashbacks

23

The Spy in Winter

6:00 P.M.: At the Majestic the caravan assembles. This is my last night in Vietnam, and although it is the custom at the end of a long television expedition for all to join in a festive dinner, I am trying hard to avoid it. A television crew is, for a week or so, an extended family, and this family with its minders has become an extended colony. I am determined to be alone, make notes, finish a paperback novel that I have been dawdling over for days. It is Julian Barnes's *Flaubert's Parrot,* and it has been providing great late-night pleasure. A twenty-minute antidote, a lights-out escape from the memories and realities of Vietnam. Room service is on my mind.

The problem of dinner is solved by Tuan, the assistant minder. He approaches me with a piece of paper.

"Mr. Pham Xuan An will see you tonight at seven," he says. "Here is his address."

I am stunned by this turn of events. I try to fathom who made this

174

decision, how it was made. I stare at the offered address. It is in the northern part of the city, near the highway to Bien Hoa.

I thank Tuan for his efforts, feeling slightly sheepish about some of the muttered asides I had made about his competence.

"One other thing, I would like to see Pham Xuan An alone. I do not need any translation."

Miss Mai leaves the decision to Tuan. "No problem, no problem. There will be a driver to take you to his house."

Tuan seems extremely relieved to be excluded from a conversation that could possibly damage a promising career.

I ask Patti Hassler to join me. I do not want to make notes when I meet with An. There is something unnerving about having someone scribble while you talk. A tape recorder is even more intimidating. But I want an observant witness to this reunion. I want every detail remembered.

We are driving through the Phu Nhuan District of Ho Chi Minh City. It is, as it was, a mixture of grand and not-so-grand villas separated by more modest houses. The main thoroughfare, the old highway to Bien Hoa, has been renamed Avenue Dien Bien Phu. We turn onto a street of small villas, of the kind occupied by middle-level U.S. embassy personnel during the war. Each is protected by a cement wall, with iron gates across the entrance. We creep along the curb looking for number 214.

Pham Xuan An is standing at the open iron gates, a pair of German shepherds flanking him. An and his beloved dogs. He would take them everywhere. He used to have his morning coffee at the Continental Palace, and always the big black snout of a German shepherd poked out from under his table.

He walks toward me, arms outstretched, and uncharacteristically for a Vietnamese, he embraces me.

An has changed very little. He is sixty-two, but he looked that old twenty years ago. Then he might have been described as wiry; today he is emaciated, almost cadaverous. He is wearing a white shirt, dark

175

trousers, and enormous heavy horn-rimmed glasses that make him look like a certified intellectual of the kind you see hanging out in cafés on the fringes of the Sorbonne. He takes them off when he talks and slips them on when he listens.

We are seated in the living room, which also serves as An's study. On a table in a corner is an old Olivetti Lettera 32 portable typewriter. There are floor-to-ceiling glass-covered bookcases filled to overflowing with English, French, and Vietnamese titles. There is a neat disorder to the room . . . piles of newspapers, books lying open on the shelves, the disorder that would indicate a preoccupied mind, not a sloppy one. There is a nice musty smell, the smell of paper quietly disintegrating in the Asian dampness.

There is a sofa and two easy chairs, and on a low table separating them, An has set out glasses, a bowl of ice, and a bottle of White Horse whiskey.

"You know, you are still a mystery. People are still unsure about who you were working for. What's the truth?"

He laughs. "The truth? Which truth? One truth is that for ten years I was a staff correspondent for *Time* magazine and before that Reuters. The other truth is that I joined the movement in 1944 and in one way or another have been part of it ever since. Two truths . . . both truths are true."

I read somewhere that the North, the Vietcong, had two hundred thousand agents active in the South during the war. I ask An how he managed to keep his identities separate.

"I am not sure. I am very lucky I didn't go insane. The identities weren't the problem. The identities were very easy. Loyalty was the problem. I learned about loyalty at university in the United States. To me, in a certain way, loyalty is a totally American idea."

An had been given a State Department scholarship to the United States in the late fifties. After university he traveled across the country, staying in peoples' homes, ending his time abroad in Orange

176

County, California, with a job on a local newspaper. He now jokes: "When I was in California I was the only Vietnamese in Orange County. I understand three hundred thousand have now taken my place."

The conversation rambles. He is anxious to know about old friends. Especially Frank McCulloch, who was *Time* bureau chief in Saigon, and Richard Clurman, who, during An's years at *Time,* was chief of correspondents, based in New York.

"McCulloch taught me everything about honest journalism. He taught me about 'getting it right.' That was his main concern. Tell him whatever I did, I did not let him down on that. I never planted a story; I was not part of any disinformation campaign. The best friends I had were at *Time.* David Greenway and other reporters taught me about friendship. Clurman demonstrated what loyalty is. Everyone in the bureau was frightened of Clurman, but when there were problems, they turned to him for help. He never let anyone down. When we lost people, when someone was killed, Clurman didn't send his sympathies; he came himself."

Frank McCulloch is now the managing editor of the *San Francisco Examiner*; David Greenway is with *The Boston Globe*; and Richard Clurman writes books and is chairman of the board of the Columbia University Media in Society Seminars.

The talk turns to Robert Shaplen, who had covered Vietnam for more than thirty years for *The New Yorker.* He died of cancer six months ago. Shaplen's Vietnamese reporter, Nguyen Hung Vuong, and An were inseparable. Vuong was a squat, intense, sour-looking man. Together they were the Mutt and Jeff of Vietnamese political minutiae . . . a two-man repository of all the intrigues, petty bickering, corruption, gossip, dirt, plotting, and grand designs of the little kings we created, the tin-pots we overthrew, the might-have-beens and never-wuzzes. In the dim forty-watt glow of An's study, I reflect on all that . . . all that scholarship of theirs that we called upon all those years ago. So important then, so utterly useless now. Vuong

177

died of cancer, too, in 1986, in lonely exile in Virginia. An and I raise a glass in silent toast.

"How did it start?" I ask.

"It was the most natural thing. In 1944 the Japanese were still here. I joined the Viet Minh along with most of my classmates. It was not a matter of choice; it was the only thing to do. We were patriots. Then, when the French came back, nothing had really changed, just the enemy. I did nothing very brave; I ran a few errands.

"The real work started in 1960, when I was working for Reuters. I held the rank of regimental commander. I never wore a uniform, of course . . . I never carried a weapon. During the years with *Time* I was made a colonel."

"What did they expect of you?"

"The same thing *Time* expected, only in greater detail. I had access to all the ARVN bases and the commanders. My superiors wanted to know the strengths of various units. They wanted estimates of the capabilities of commanders . . . who was corrupt and who was corruptible. They wanted all the political stuff, the same stuff you guys wanted."

"Did they want you to place stories in *Time?*"

"No. They were clever enough to know how easy that kind of thing is to spot. They told me over and over to do nothing that might compromise my job. A couple of times I had to sit on very good stories because my source would have been too obvious. The only time I risked doing anything like that was during the Paris peace talks. We, *Time,* had a series of great scoops."

"How easy was it to pass on information?"

"In Saigon we had a liaison system. I would just pass it on. I tried to avoid putting anything on paper. Then every few months I would disappear for a couple of days. It wasn't unusual for me to do that for *Time.* My commanders preferred the long debriefings. We met in a couple of places, but mainly in the Ho Bo forest."

Morley Safer

The Ho Bo forest is about ten miles northwest of Saigon. It was under almost constant attack by the American 25th Infantry Division.

"One time, it was during a Tet truce, I was on my way back to Saigon, when one side or the other—I'm not sure—started shooting, and I got caught in the middle. I spent two days and two nights in a ditch. I really thought it was all over for me. I thought, what a rotten way to die, the victim of a truce."

As he talks An leans over, his elbows on his knees, a Lucky Strike dangling from his bony fingers. He speaks with an easy grace, with the mannerisms of a donnish poet. He makes no demands on his visitors. He is guilty of no special pleading.

"Were you frightened that you might be discovered?"

"Constantly. I was terrified. You know there were rumors in the sixties that I was working for the CIA. I did my best not to discourage those tales. I thought it gave me a little more protection. Later, of course, it became a threat. We worked in very close security. I don't think more than half a dozen people knew of my activities. In the early seventies, when things started going badly for the government, I was worried that when the collapse came there wouldn't be time to explain to some kid from the countryside, armed with an AK-47, that I was a colonel in his army. I used to tell people they'll probably kill me and roast my dog."

His explanations do not clarify; they deepen the mystery of the man. The puzzle becomes an enigma. Sitting a few feet away in the semigloom, his eyes enlarged by those ridiculous heavy glasses, he goes out of focus. How many more layers are there? How much more is there to be told in this friendly confession?

In his book, *The Fall of Saigon,* David Butler describes An's gallantry in helping Dr. Tran Kim Tuyen to escape. Tuyen was one of the most highly placed CIA agents in Vietnam. An incurable plotter who had worked for and against the Thieu government, on the last day of Saigon he was still at it, trying to

179

make a deal with the Buddhist hierarchy to form a new government.

Tuyen would have been a priority target for the Vietcong. He had organized and presided over Diem's secret police and, with American assistance, had set up Saigon's first intelligence network aimed at the North. In the confusion preceding the collapse of the city he had missed two different flights that the CIA had arranged for him and his family. His wife and children managed to leave through friends at the British embassy, but on the last day of the war he had no one to turn to but Pham Xuan An. An shoved him in his car and drove through a collapsing Saigon to an American apartment building . . . bluffed his way past a guard, forced open the iron gates, and ordered Tuyen to go to the roof. There is a picture from that last day of figures silhouetted on a rooftop stairway that reaches up to an American helicopter. The figure on the bottom step is Tuyen. An is not in the picture. He stayed.

There could be nothing more significant to this act than an unwillingness to stand by and do nothing. An's unwillingness to let agony occur when he had the wit and compassion to prevent it. And the courage too. An is a patriot, I decide, one of the genuine few I have known.

I do not press him further. His answer would only reveal another layer.

The speculation about An's activities was red meat to Arnaud de Borchgrave, who years ago took up the cry that American journalism was infiltrated by communist disinformation. In 1981 he testified before Senator Jeremiah Denton's subcommittee on security and terrorism that An was an agent whose mission was to disinform the Western press.

De Borchgrave is a former senior editor of *Newsweek* and is now the editor in chief of the *Washington Times,* the newspaper controlled by the Reverend Sun Myung Moon's Unification Church. De Borchgrave had a brilliant career at *Newsweek,* marred only slightly by an ego so enormous that in his last years at the magazine he had taken to referring to himself in the third person, as in "Arnaud believes there will be another war in the Middle East." Because of his small stature and quite accurate claim to be of Belgian royal blood, he was known around *Newsweek* as "the short count." He is a bullet-headed, feisty little man who in the sixties and seventies liked to collect wars and was constantly boasting of how many he had covered. If William F. Buckley is the Torquemada of American right-wing journalism, Arnaud de Borchgrave is its Jake LaMotta. He is firmly convinced that *Time* unwittingly published An's communist-inspired stories, without offering any evidence at all of actual disinformation.

Douglas Pike, one of the few Americans who had any real understanding at all of the Vietcong, believes An is "scrupulously moral in the traditional Confucian ethic."

Whatever he was, whatever he did in the past, he is a dignified and decent man, a believer still in a small, honorable destiny for his country. I do not think of him as a Communist, though he is still a loyal party member. I can't even think of him as a Nationalist. It is a perverted word that too often masks grandiose and ugly possibilities.

"What happened that day, after everyone left?"

"Bob Shaplen gave me the keys to his room at the Continental. So did a couple of the other correspondents. I went home, picked up my mother and moved into the hotel. I knew it would be safer there. My mother was also very ill, and I thought it would be easier to look after her in the hotel. My wife and children had already left on the flight that *Time* arranged.

"My worst fear was that they would use rockets and artillery on the city. An artillery attack would have killed thousands. I had seen what happened in 1968 during Tet, and I couldn't face that again. It was seeing the children, that was the worst of it. If I saw that again, I knew I would go insane.

181

"It was clear to me that Saigon would not be defended, but I feared they would not believe me. I could barely believe it."

"Why did you stay? Did you want to see it through?"

"I suppose so. Something like that. I think it is difficult for an outsider to understand and just as difficult for me to explain. Maybe I don't understand why. I knew we had to get rid of the foreigners. Even the foreigners I love so much. Maybe I thought I could help rebuild the country. Even if I had wanted to go, there was my mother. She was too old and too ill to travel."

"We have a saying in Vietnamese: You can find a new wife. You can have another son. You cannot replace a mother. So I stayed. At first I thought I would find someone to look after her and join my family in France or the States. But they made it clear to me that they would not let me leave."

There is a look of great weariness in his face. The spy in winter. The dutiful elderly son who chose loyalty over freedom. The first year of "liberation" was spent in a camp . . . not a reeducation camp, he explains, but a special camp near Hanoi for "friends" who might have been contaminated by too close a relationship with the Americans.

"It wasn't hard labor; it was lectures, long lectures, mainly dealing with Party theory. People felt I needed a brush-up after all those years of working for the Americans. When I returned to Saigon, my wife and children came back. I wanted them back, but I left the decision to them."

All four of An's children are in their twenties now. His oldest son works as a translator, having studied English and Russian at the Foreign Language Institute in Moscow. Another son is an engineer and still another a psychologist. An's daughter will soon graduate from medical school.

"Why did the revolution fail?"

"There are many reasons. So many mistakes were made just out of sheer ignorance. Like every revolution we called it a *people's* revolution, but of course the *people* were the first to suffer."

182

We had talked of the homeless earlier. An looked embarassed, as though he somehow was responsible for them, had helped bring on their calamity. I suppose, in a way, he had, but now has the decency to feel shame. All that talk of liberation twenty, thirty, forty years ago, all the plotting and all the bodies produced this impoverished, broken-down country. Revolution as punishment, liberation as a grandiose denial of possibilities.

"As long as the people sleep in the streets, the revolution was lost," An says. "It is not that the leaders are cruel men, but the effect of paternalism and discredited economic theory is the same."

"Aren't you worried about talking so bluntly? Isn't it dangerous?"

"Everyone knows how I feel. I make no secret of it. I never have. During the Thieu government everyone knew exactly what I thought of those thieves. I'm too old to change." He laughs. "I'm too old to shut up."

"What about the reforms? I get the feeling that something is beginning to happen. Am I wrong?"

"No, not wrong, just too optimistic. It's the American disease."

"I'm not American, An, I'm Canadian."

He laughs. "I'm sorry, I forgot. Being a Canadian makes you less optimistic . . . but still, probably, too optimistic. I wish the reforms represented a genuine reevaluation, a genuine *perestroika*. Maybe I am too pessimistic. That's a disease that is easy to catch in this country."

"But the way people, especially in the South, responded to the reforms. Surely the leadership is smart enough to get the message."

"The way people responded. That's what breaks my heart. To see that spirit going crazy with delight over a few economic reforms. It gives a hint of what the possibilities are for this damn country if we could have not just peace, but freedom."

"Do they watch you?"

"Yes, just like in the days of Thieu. They watch me out of habit now, not because they expect to learn anything. They know everything there is to know about me."

183

"Will they let you leave?"

"I don't know. I'm not sure I want to. At the very least I would like my children to go to the States to study."

The bottle of White Horse is almost empty. The three of us have been sipping steadily through the evening. Patti sits at her end of the sofa, being the perfect fly on the wall. But clearly she is touched by An's passion and honesty and intrigued by the paradox . . . that talent for slipping out of focus. I ask An: "Do you regret what you did, now that you've seen the results?"

"I hate that question. I have asked it of myself a thousand times. But I hate the answer more. No. No regrets. I had to do it. This peace that I fought for may be crippling this country, but the war was killing it. As much as I love the United States, it had no right here. The Americans had to be driven out of Vietnam one way or another. We must sort this place out ourselves."

Poor An. He occupies that no-man's-land called the middle ground or, depending on the generation, the third force. No place for a sensitive soul. Historically of course it has been occupied only by sensitive souls. If Graham Greene had looked at Vietnam in another way, he might have written *The Quiet Vietnamese,* with Pham Xuan An as his model.

An is neither apologetic about the cause he served, nor does he rail against it. His is not a case of a "God that Failed." Unlike Arthur Koestler and other reformed addicts of Marxism, I doubt that An ever was a believer. A god did not fail him. Men did.

I suspect he did what was for him the natural thing, not especially courageous. There is a distinction between a spy and a traitor. For him to have served Nguyen Van Thieu would have been an act of betrayal. As for Americans, he was capable of separating his feelings for the Americans he worked with from the cause the American government was pursuing. In fact what he wanted for his country were the things Americans already had. This is what I believe, while

184

knowing it is impossible to fathom the complexities of another's mind and motives.

My suspicion is that he made no great definitive decision about himself, politics, or his country. I think that he, like most men, kept taking what seemed to be the logical next step. Unlike most men, there was a minimum of self-interest involved. There are no saints, just people with varying degrees of selflessness.

It is past nine o'clock. I ask An if he will join us for dinner at La Bibliothèque, the best restaurant in all of Vietnam, owned by a woman named Madam Dai, who is somewhat of a mystery herself, but a fairly noisy, chatty one. "Thank you, no," he says and with a great grin on his face, continues: "I don't like going there; I think it's too rich for my blood."

An walks us out to the car; the dogs swarm around his feet. "You've led a couple of interesting lives," I tell him. "Why don't you write it all down. It would be a fascinating book. An important one too."

He slips off the glasses and looks up at the night sky. I can barely see his face in the dark, but I hear a small trill of sad laughter. "All the years that I was a reporter," he says, "all those years, no one told me what to write. I am too old to learn some new rules about what can be said and what cannot. I'm afraid my reporting days are over."

He embraces me, shakes my hand. "Please tell all my friends you saw me," he says. "Tell Clurman and McCulloch and Charlie Mohr, especially. Tell them I am doing well. Well enough." Charlie Mohr, first for *Time,* then *The New York Times,* was one of the first American reporters to cover Vietnam's agonies in the early sixties, and among the most perceptive.*

*On returning to the United States I called both Clurman and McCulloch, both of whom were extremely touched that An remembers them so fondly. To my regret, I never reached Charlie Mohr. He died on his sixtieth birthday in June 1989.

185

I promise to make the calls. "I really want to come back, find another story here. I'll come back and buy you that dinner."

"That would be nice, Morley. That would be very nice. But I think the next one of the guys that I see will probably be Shaplen. Shaplen and Vuong."

I can't see his face, only his silhouette against the light of the living-room window. The long bony arm waves a farewell, and the dogs bark us out of the driveway.

24

The House on Nguyen Du Street

9:00 P.M.: There is no sign on the house on Nguyen Du Street, nothing to indicate that it is a restaurant. From the outside it is a nondescript villa that could be the residence of a minor colonial official or a lesser bishop serving in the Basilica of Our Lady of Peace, just around the corner. The building is the home of a woman known only as Madam Dai. It is also the restaurant La Bibliothèque. It has been recommended by David Greenway, who, apart from his courage and tenacity as a journalist, has a wonderful talent for ferreting out whatever small comforts may be available in some of the world's most forsaken cities. He shares this knowledge with great enthusiasm.

To walk into the house is to step through a looking glass into colonial Saigon. A cool, high-ceilinged respite from the heat and worldly utilitarian priorities of the People's Republic outside. The hall and two dining rooms are lined with glass-fronted bookcases.

Most of the books are French legal texts—colonial case law, rec-

187

ords of trials, all the essentials of a good-sized law library, all neatly stacked and bound in morocco.

The tables are covered in crisp white linen, and wherever there is space there are pots of freshly cut flowers. A fat lazy gray cat sprawls lustily across a windowsill. Two smaller ones stalk the hall seeking largesse dropped by waiters treading between kitchen and dining rooms.

Madam Dai approaches. She is a tiny woman of seventy-two with a memory of great beauty in her face. She could be Miss Mai, grown old. Miss Mai had said she hates the place. "The cats make me break out."

Madam Dai greets Patti and me in French and shows us to the table next to the gray cat's window. She is still a striking woman. Her hair is pulled back in a chignon, and she is wearing a dark blue silk shirt and black silk pajama trousers. I tell her I have a vague memory of meeting her during the war.

"It is quite possible; I met many journalists."

"You were a deputy . . . a representative to the National Assembly. Did we not meet at the French embassy?"

"Perhaps. I was a deputy for ten years. I was many things in those days."

She drifts off, stopping at other tables, being the solicitous hostess. There is a sad air of a duchess fallen on difficult times, forced by cruel circumstance to take in paying guests. She fills a wineglass, asks if the shrimp is to the taste of the diner. Most of the guests are foreign. Diplomats mostly. She fits her manner to the mood of each legation. At a round table ten Australians are carrying on raucously. With enough beer Aussies can turn a churchyard into a Melbourne pub, and usually do. She joins them briefly and lets out a deep throaty laugh at a no doubt tasteful outback joke.

She returns to our table and asks if we would like the French or the Vietnamese dinner.

"Because of the hour, I suggest you try the Vietnamese. It is a mélange, a mixture of dishes. You will enjoy it. We agree. Perhaps you would like some wine. We have just received a shipment of an excellent Côtes du Rhone."

After so many meals in the dim gray light of dining halls that socialist revolutionaries all over the world seem to favor, the warm paneling and candlelight of Madam Dai's are like a very good dream. The dreamlike quality is enhanced by her chief waitress, an elderly Chinese woman who has the look of an old family retainer. The odd thing is, she speaks English in an almost overcultivated British accent, of the kind used by Bond Street salespeople. It is an Oriental Fawlty Towers without the spillage.

Dinner arrives and it is extraordinary. A fish soup that could have been flown in from the Vieux Port in Marseilles, followed by a triple-tiered tray heaped with venison and fresh mint rolled into rice paper, accompanied by a sauce, the ingredients of which have been so subtly mingled it defies all attempts at identification. On the next tier are skewers of chicken pieces grilled and dipped into more unidentifiable Vietnamese herbs . . . and on the bottom tier, grilled shrimp in yet another sauce so light that it is impossible to tell where the shrimp ends and the sauce begins.

The wine is as advertised and so is the French cheese that is urged on us. That is followed by fresh pineapple. Madam Dai joins us and offers a cognac on the house.

"Calvados?"

"Of course."

I try my best to draw her out. How does she manage to maintain this standard in impoverished, socialist Vietnam?

"It is not difficult; I have friends who assist me."

The more details I have of the life of this remarkable woman, the more puzzling she becomes.

She was educated in France and became the first woman trial lawyer in Vietnam. She was a confidante and press secretary to Madam Nhu, the sister-in-law of President Diem, as cruel and im-

189

placable a woman as I have ever talked to. Madam Nhu described the suicide of Buddhist monks opposed to her husband's and brother-in-law's régime as "barbecues started with cheap American gasoline."

In the middle sixties Madam Dai started the Vietnam Women's Movement, a society of talented Francophile women like herself. Its goal was to influence public policy. It was extremely anticommunist, and on that platform she was elected to the National Assembly. She had married quite young, to a leading Saigon physician, but maintained an open and scandalous affair with Nguyen Van Tho, Diem's minister of information. She has two children, both of whom live in the United States.

Then her story becomes murky, and she does nothing to clarify it. Did she, as is rumored, totally misread the intention of the North Vietnamese and Vietcong and believe that the South would remain a separate state, run by some neutralist coalition—which meant a lot of her old friends? Or did she just wait too long to try to get out? Did she, as is also rumored, welcome the collapse of her friend General Thieu as a way of wiping clean some enormous debts she'd piled up trying to maintain a certain way of life? Revolutions do have their positive effects. Or is the rumor she favors most of all the true story? That for years she provided a safe haven for a nest of spies and Vietcong infiltrators, in this very house, and is therefore a minor heroine of the revolution whose reward is the right to offer decent food in pleasant surroundings?

There is, as I believe is always the case in Vietnam, some small element of truth in each of the possibilities.

Madam Dai sips her mineral water across from me, a look of amusement playing across her face. I thank her, pay the check, which is remarkably modest, and we get up to leave.

"You must come back, and please tell your friends about my establishment," she says. "I expect soon to expand the menu, to offer a better wine list."

As we leave I look back. She has joined a man, an Englishman,

190

who is dining alone. He is of an age and demeanor that would qualify him perfectly for the job of queen's messenger, the grandiose title the British Foreign Service gives to the men who carry the diplomatic bag. You will find them, usually on British Airways flights, occupying two first-class seats. One for the man; one for the bag handcuffed to his wrist. The bag no customs dare open.

Madam Dai and the man I presume to be her majesty's most excellent messenger are deep in discussion, practically nose to nose.

25

The Giacometti
Buddha

Ho Chi Minh City, January 26, 7:00 A.M.:   The sun is well up in
the sky over Ho Chi Minh City.

This is my last day, and although I have completed everything I
had to do for the television project, I have an uneasy feeling of
business left unfinished. I do not understand and probably never will
the grip that this place has on me. I have tried very hard not to make
this just a sentimental journey.

I stare out my window over the scraggy rooftops and their sagging
clotheslines, jumbles of litter, and the curious, highly individual stick
figures of television aerials.

Although I am not due to leave for the airport for another nine
hours, I pack my bags. I pick up *Flaubert's Parrot* from the night table
to take down to breakfast, then change my mind. Julian Barnes's
literary clevernesses are better left for the long haul on Air France.
I toss it on top of my shoulder bag and go downstairs to the Majestic
terrace for coffee.

There is a river road that snakes along the waterfront and through the port of Saigon. The section in front of the Majestic is divided by a grassy median, which at night is occupied by the homeless. They are gone now except for a one-legged man who is setting up shop for the day.

He is shirtless, wearing only a pair of dark blue shorts, from which his stump, calloused and misshapen, protrudes. His tools consist of a bicycle pump, some cut-up pieces of inner tube, a pot of glue, and a GI steel helmet filled with water. He is as thin and slow-moving as an Ethiopian you'd see on the evening news.

He is one of the thousands of ARVN soldiers, that wretched army that was damned by the victors, abandoned by its allies, and royally and continuously screwed by its commanders. They pick away at jobs like this man's or congregate in front of the basilica trying to catch the attention of foreigners, slipping them notes for long-gone Americans they think might be able to help.

The man squats blinking in the morning sun, a crippled Gandhi whose hope soars no higher than the pavement. The fervent wish for a shard of glass to find a home in a cyclist's tire.

The coffee arrives with French bread still warm from the oven. My thoughts turn to Charles Collingwood, who, for all the sangfroid he liked to present to the world, would be moved to tears and genuine charity by the sight before me. He never lived here, but he came here regularly to report at length and with perhaps an excess of caution the course of the war. We argued about it, sometimes with great passion, but never with rancor. Collingwood would never let it happen. He would steer the hostilities to dinner or high-stakes poker, usually both.

He was scrupulous to keep his own reservations about the war clear of his reporting and won and kept the trust of everyone who knew him. During the 1968 Paris peace talks, all the world's press was chasing after Averell Harriman, chief American negotiator, convinced that he was making unofficial nighttime contact with his

North Vietnamese and Vietcong counterparts. When reporters finally caught up with him after a car chase through Paris, they discovered him having dinner with Collingwood.

During the Second World War he was given the nickname "the Duke." Many years later I was having a drink at the Ritz Bar in Paris when an old woman and her companion approached me. She touched my arm and said, "Send my love to the Duke." There was no question which duke. There was only one. The woman was Janet Flanner, *The New Yorker*'s resident interpreter of the political, social, and private lives of the French and author of *Paris Was Yesterday*.

Collingwood was one of "Murrow's Boys," the archetypal one. When for various reasons he slid from popularity within the comintern that ran CBS News, he did so with the grace of a champion. He railed against neither fate nor his agent. His interests ranged from conflicts within the Han dynasty to thoroughbred bloodlines. He was honest and above all fair. He was a scholar when broadcasting no longer wanted one, amused more than appalled by the contract-crazed chorus girls and boys who've taken over the podium.

He died in 1985 of a wonderful excess of living. In the last days of his life, barely able to speak, imprisoned by a variety of hospital tubing, he had me read him the morning line from Aqueduct.

I fear I am reaching an age where it becomes difficult to resist the instinct to sentimentalize this craft. That instinct is enhanced by the memories of lasting friendships made in ludicrous and dangerous moments in places that had become unhinged.

Charles and I and Ha Thuc Can, if he were in town, would sneak away to the museum in Saigon for a quiet hour away from the Vietnamese intrigues and the American statistics. Although it housed the relics of even bloodier times, it did represent a form of stability. There are no tomorrows in museums, only thousands and thousands of yesterdays frozen in curatorial aspic. Tomorrow tends to jump up and bite you in the ass. Yesterday is a good dog.

There was an ancient wooden Buddha at the museum that had

been dug up out of the delta mud. It was well over six feet high, but the worms and rot had eaten away its sides, elongating the figure, giving it a tortured appearance. Where the wood was once smooth, it now had a rough cast. It was very modern looking, but unlike almost all modern sculpture, this withered figure jarred the viewer. Collingwood nicknamed it the Giacometti Buddha.

Let it be a sentimental journey. I ask the driver to take me to the museum for a small homage to Messrs. Collingwood, Giacometti, and Buddha.

The museum is on Nguyen Binh Khiem Street, in a magnificent park that is also home to the Ho Chi Minh City Zoo. The admission system is a mystifying example of socialist planning and employment practices. Three women stand shoulder to shoulder behind a counter on the pavement outside the park's gates. The first takes my money—only pennies—the second issues a ticket to the park; the third issues a ticket to the museum. A fourth woman stands a few feet away and punches the park ticket; behind her a fifth punches the museum ticket.

The forecourt of the museum has been decked out with bunting and portable stalls. The festival of Tet will be celebrated in a few days. Vietnamese families go into debt this time of the year buying presents for family members, especially the children, and special foods and treats for everyone. It is much more than simply a new year's celebration. The Vietnamese do not make much of individual birthdays. Instead they celebrate everyone's birthday during Tet. The precise date of death is much more significant here.

Most of the stalls are selling boxes of chocolates and jars of preserved fruit in a sickly sweet sauce, an undrinkable liquid the Vietnamese call wine, and fancy boxes of perfumed soap. One stall has a display of children's goods, various items of clothing and balloons, and an array of cheap plastic toys. One stall is selling little boys' soldier hats and swords. They are made from cardboard packing cases and still bear the repeated imprint "Hitachi" all over them.

195

Inside the museum a sixth ticket taker demands to see my paper-work.

Somehow the museum seems much grander than I remember it, cleaner, better illuminated. There is a large golden bust of Ho Chi Minh in the rotunda, with a legend describing him as the savior of the nation, but beyond that the museum remains politically neutral. By contrast a Chinese museum will not display so much as an arrow-head without a ripping polemic.

It would go something like:

Arrowhead. Early Chai Ching period. This implement demon-strates the instinctive ingenuity of the exploited masses of workers, soldiers, and peasants in designing weapons and tools for their cruel Ming masters, who were the forerunners of today's deviant pseudo-Communists, the pernicious running dogs for foreign im-perialists of every stripe.

The little white cards describing in English, French, and Viet-namese each of the displays are written in a stiff academic prose, giving only the approximate age of the artifact and the location and date of its discovery.

Twenty-five years ago the curator was a man I knew only as Dr. Quan. He must have been in his eighties then. He had the look and manner of a Confucian scholar whose ideas had been corrupted by a French academician. He had a wispy Ho Chi Minh beard and wore a loose smock over trousers that were much too big for him. I doubted he ever left the museum. He had only the vaguest of ideas that there was a war going on outside and asked me one day who all these foreigners were who spoke no French. He looked puzzled when I explained that there was an army of three hundred thousand Americans in the country.

"My God," he said. "Who on earth are they fighting?"

He regarded his artifacts as though they were wonderfully behaved visitors from whom he would learn something new every day. His

196

favorites lived alone in their own vitrine, quite aloof from the over-done, Chinese-influenced stone-and-wooden carvings. They were a collection of Roman coins, buckles, and amulets that were dug up sometime in the twenties in the Mekong delta near what is now the Cambodian border.

"The Romans," he would say, his parchment face beaming with pride, "I still do not have their full story."

Scholars are still stumped by the find. Could it be that the Romans were here as some kind of expeditionary force, and after a brief encounter with Vietnamese stubbornness decided that the British, French, and Germans were more malleable savages? If so, they were the quickest learners of all of Vietnam's rambunctious houseguests.

I do not know what happened to Dr. Quan. The fact that the museum suffered only minor pillaging makes me believe that he probably died peacefully here among his old friends. I trust that his new masters did not try to reeducate him. If they did, they would have had to begin sometime around the second century and would be old men themselves by the time they got to the third.

I drift over to the vitrine. The Romans are still there under glass, the emperor's profiles smiling enigmatically at each other. Not far away, looking quite disdainful at these European interlopers, is the Giacometti Buddha. Charles would be pleased.

I return to the Majestic, taking a roundabout route through Cho-lon, the old Chinese quarter west of the city. The mission is to purchase a small metal trunk. The caravan has bought an excess of knickknacks, pottery, chopping boards, and straw baskets from the Danang market. I, of course, am the worst offender. I have a base-ment in New York and a barn in Connecticut that are repositories of thirty-five years of buying the useless and near-useless products of six continents' schlock-meisters. There is enough stuff of question-able taste to furnish a suite for Donald and Ivana Trump.

Cholon is like most Chinese cities, only more so. A street, or at least each side of any street, has its unofficially declared art, craft, or

197

profession. A whole block of Cholon has nothing but plumbing parts, bathtubs, bidets, and toilets and their attendant pipes, elbows, and faucets in conditions that range from old to new, from shattered to renovated. There are kiosks heaped high with washers and connectors. The pavement is crowded with men carrying wrenches, some walking determinedly to an assignment, others standing chatting, discussing, no doubt, the good old days of French plumbing. Some squat, smoking, staring off into some private middle distance. There are streets of flower sellers, wholesale and retail, who in truth have only one price. It is the problem of the customer to discover it. One street has storefront after storefront of furniture under construction. There is the good pungent smell of oil-based stain and freshly cut wood. Stylistically, each craftsman's work is identical—Chinese Chippendale stained exactly the same shade of burnt sienna.

What is missing are the coffin makers. Twenty years ago it was one of Vietnam's growth industries. There must have been hundreds of them in Saigon, and even the smallest hamlet had at least one retail outlet store. So far I have only spotted one, on the road to Cu Chi.

We turn in to the street of the trunk makers. Again each establishment is both factory and retail outlet, and each shop's product is precisely the same as its neighbor's, constructed in exactly the same aluminum sheet metal.

We choose the busiest one, on the theory shared by New Yorkers and lemmings that *this* must be *the* place. The front of the shop is stacked with finished goods of every capacity, from attaché case to steamer trunk. Every case but the smallest has two pairs of wheels, and each bears the name and what must be the potential new address of its owner. They are painted on the case in immaculate hand lettering, with great sweeping serifs, all in the same red with yellow shading, the national colors of the hated puppet regime. Names and places like "Huynh Than Pham, Winnipeg, Manitoba" and "Thi Binh Minh, San Jose, California." Vietnam, under some pressure from the outside and embarrassed by the horrible ordeals the boat people suffer just trying to get out of the place, has agreed to allow a certain amount of legal emigration. It is called the Orderly Departure Plan—ODP. It is both a corrupt and painfully slow process. The owners of these cases must be among the lucky ones who have been given a date and a visa. Or perhaps they simply live in hope, cases at the ready for the day the visa comes through. Half a nation, perhaps, living with its bags packed.

The owner of the establishment is a tall reed of a man much distracted by the good business he is doing. Behind him half a dozen employees are working feverishly, tapping at the aluminum, bending and riveting the supports. I get his attention and hold up my hands to demonstrate the approximate dimensions. He reaches down for a yardstick, measuring the thin air between my outstretched arms, and writes it on his palm. I switch dimensions to give depth and width, and this air too is measured and recorded. He writes a price on his palm and I nod agreement. "When?" I ask, using the international semaphore for such a question, which is to point a finger at one's watch. He responds by holding up two fingers. I reply by drawing a clock face on my hand, count off two hours and fix the hands at one P.M. He shakes his head no, takes me by the hand to the back of the shop, and, on a huge lurid Chinese calendar, counts off two weeks.

I shake my head no and add for emphasis a lot of hand gesturing designed to say, "That is not good enough, sir. I must have this case this afternoon."

I take his shrug to mean, "Tough luck, pal. That's the best I can do."

I put on my most pleading face, and with gestures I indicate that I can live without the hand lettering and wheels.

He replies with a sour grin and a palm thrust out, which I interpret as: "Okay, pal, I'll do my best. How about a deposit?"

The deal is struck, and as we leave I see him at his guillotine slicing sheet metal to the more or less correct dimensions. Louis Vuitton in old army shorts and rubber tire flip-flops.

At the hotel I make preparations to leave. Patti agrees to go back

199

to Mr. Vuitton to collect the trunk. There are a few other bits of unfinished business. From the crew I cadge the last copy of Neil Sheehan's *A Bright Shining Lie* and inscribe it to Pham Xuan An.

> To An:
> Who so far has led two painful and exciting lives. May you live the third one in contentment.

I ask Patti to deliver it after I leave, along with a bottle of White Horse to replace the one we destroyed. For reasons I cannot quite comprehend, I do not want to see him again, certainly not with both of us aware that it is my last hour in Vietnam. I do not want to remind him so poignantly how easy it is for his old friends to come and go. *Glasnost* and *doi moi* exist, but only for the foreign and the privileged. I always felt slightly guilty leaving Vietnam, if only for four or five days of rest in Hong Kong. Vietnamese friends would wish me well, but with pain and envy written large in their faces. When people in the old CBS bureau called the plane out of Vietnam the "Freedom Bird," the Vietnamese staff would visibly wince at the phrase, at the casualness of the arrival and departure of we colonial-ists-one-step-removed. As if their tragedy, their national hemorrhage was nothing more than a stop on a Disney tour. A stop that, however exciting, goes on a little too long. "Freedom Bird." It has the ring of an adolescent description of the bus ride home from a tedious summer camp.

In the lobby of the Majestic, Miss Mai is getting anxious. It is her job to see me through the airport formalities and tucked neatly into the Air France flight.

"You must not be late," she says. "The airport can be a real hassle."

I point out that it is only two o'clock, that the plane is not due to leave until six.

"Please, believe me. Four hours is not too much time. International departure is a zoo."

Morley Safer

"I have one errand. I will be back in an hour."

She seems distressed by this. Heaven knows what the punishment is for losing a foreigner. "I will come with you; it's my a . . . my fault if you miss that plane. The driver will take us."

"No, Mai, I would rather go alone. I think you would be happier if I go alone . . . it is not far. I don't need the driver."

This slightly ominous statement produces a cheery smile but the hard eyes. It is a look I have not seen for days.

"Okay, but please, one hour."

I had promised Frank, the ex-Mike force trooper, that I would come by to meet his wife. The shop is an alcove no more than four feet square. There are a few pieces of lacquer on the shelves, and on the pavement there is an easel with rattan bags hanging from hooks. Frank and his wife are standing in front of the easel, very formally, almost at attention. She introduces herself and presents me with her card:

Arts and Crafts
Ceramic—Lacquer—Bamboo
JEANNETTE DIEM QUYNH

She is a woman in her forties with very delicate features. Her skin has a weather-beaten look to it, and her eyes are the saddest I have ever seen. She is wearing a flowered Chinese smock and trousers. They are neatly pressed but faded, as if they have been washed and ironed every day.

"Excuse my English," she says. "It is a little broken down from disuse. My husband he say you leave today. I have letters if you would be kind enough to send them when you leave Vietnam. The stamps are so expensive."

She gives me a half-dozen letters, all with Texas addresses. She then reaches over the easel, removes a small rattan bag, and presents it.

"Please take this. It is for shopping. A small memory of Vietnam."

201

Frank, who has disappeared around the corner, returns balancing cups of coffee.

"Please stay for a moment. It is so good for Jeannette and me to speak English. It is almost like being in the States. Just to hear you talk makes us feel better. Can you be homesick for a place you've never seen?"

We are squatting on stools no more than eight inches high. The local version of what the Irish call "famine stools," perches of only slightly higher altitude than the floor—and only slightly more comfortable. Jeannette has moved off to talk to another woman, a neighboring shopkeeper, explaining, perhaps, the presence of their guest. Misery is etched deeply into Frank's face. The missing teeth make him look ancient.

"It is much worse for her," he says, nodding toward his wife. "She must work for both of us. I have made her a prisoner like me. I am marked for life and so is she as long as she stays with me. She wanted so much to have children, but during the war we decided not to have them, and after the war I was away for ten years. Now, at her age, it is not easy."

He pauses, staring at his coffee.

". . . and after the camp, after my reeducation, I do not function properly. I don't think I can help her to have a baby. Do you understand?"

"Yes, I understand."

"No, I don't mean that. Do you understand what it means to a Vietnamese to have no children?"

"Yes. I think I understand that too." I feel helpless. As if this man has been waiting decades for some stranger to listen to his story, expecting some revelation, some wise solution to his dilemma. The Americans were, after all, great problem solvers. I'm sure his captain could whistle up a helicopter or an air strike at will.

"I am sorry, Frank. I am genuinely sorry." I reach into my right pocket, the one with green, with dollars, and place a handful of bills in his hand. Thirty or forty dollars.

"For Jeannette," I say. "Something pretty for Tet."

"I cannot express very well what I feel," he says. Tears fill his eyes. "You don't know how much this money is. This is a great fortune." He makes a half-hearted attempt to give some of it back.

I think of Nguyen Van Thieu living sumptuously in the stockbroker belt of Wimbledon outside London. His evacuation along with his aides and a planeload of suitcases containing heavy metal was arranged by the CIA. What worldly goods he could not take with him had been carefully stashed in advance in blind-eyed banks.

The dreadful old Hanoi rhetoric about puppets and puppeteers seems to make perfect sense. After the battle of the Ia Drang Valley, in 1965, a colonel in the 1st Air Cavalry Division, William Lynch, said of the Vietcong: ". . . it appears the little bastards just don't have the stomach for a fight; they've had enough and bugged out."

In the big one, the big bastards had enough and bugged out . . . taking select little bastards with them. They left behind the poor and the true believers. All the promises bogus. All the death meaningless.

Frank and Jeannette shake my hand very formally. Tears are in their eyes. For a hardened people, the Vietnamese are easily touched. So are we, I guess.

26

Departure

Miss Mai is unusually quiet on the drive to Tan Son Nhut. Those blazing eyes seem hooded, idling in neutral. I suspect the cause of this reticence is, once again, the envy of our good fortune, our easy access. Wherever we are, a Freedom Bird is waiting.

At the airport she snaps: "Follow me. Stay close behind." With her magic pass in one hand and my documents in the other, she plunges into the crowd. I follow that perfect Levi Strauss-ed bottom as it wriggles toward the departure desk, like a fullback staying with his key blocker. She was right. The place is a zoo. A forest of hands is waving tickets trying desperately to get the attention of desk clerks, security guards, anyone of the dozen indifferent bureaucrats behind the barrier. When a hand is rewarded with a boarding pass the face takes on an expression of such joy that the rectangular piece of pasteboard might well be a winning lottery ticket. One thing the Vietnamese are truly incapable of achieving is Orderly Departure.

Miss Mai puts her magic pass between her teeth and vaults the

Morley Safer

departure desk. She lands, shoves the pass at a rookie security guard, throws him her neutron smile; he melts, makes the necessary five bangs of his rubber stamp, she is back a minute later with ticket, boarding pass, passport, customs document, and baggage tags.

"You can go through now," she says, face and voice still icy. "You are no longer my responsibility." We shake hands, almost solemnly.

"Thank you, Mai. Thank you, Terrifier of Colonels. Thank you, Enemy of Bureaucracy and all its running dogs. I hope your fiancé is a very strong man, and you have a long and happy marriage."

The eyes soften and the smile erupts.

"You are welcome, Stone Face. You better go now. Your Freedom Bird awaits."

I go out and up the ramp and enter cool Air France, walking through yet another looking glass. Champagne, wanted or not, is placed on the armrest. An array of current French and English newspapers is offered. Purring hostesses hang coats and fluff pillows. I stare out the windows at the squat buildings of Tan Son Nhut, back out through the looking glass, and wonder about the hold that this place, especially this city, has on a generation. My notebook from last night says: "It is difficult to imagine a more spirited people than these Vietnamese. They confound our best intentions with their cynicism and our most evil maneuvers with trust and love. . . ." I am not sure what I meant by that. Notes made past midnight ring true at the time, but they become the next day's babble.

Doors close, engines whine into life. The almost-equatorial night plummets down on Saigon. Sitting up in the hump of this hump-backed Freedom Bird, it is Saigon once again. "Ho Chi Minh City" seems too cumbersome, too polemical. The Boeing rumbles out low over the city. Weak lights wink back at us. It is time to return to *Flaubert's Parrot*. Julian Barnes reports that Flaubert borrowed the stuffed parrot from the Museum of Rouen and placed it on his worktable during the writing of *Un Coeur Simple,* where it is called "Lolou." Barnes wonders if the writer is much more than a

205

sophisticated parrot. I wonder if the writer is much more than a sophisticated stuffed parrot.

I reach down under the seat for my shoulder bag to pick up where I left off. *Flaubert's Parrot* is gone. Stolen back at the hotel!

I settle back instead with the *International Herald Tribune,* and I find myself smiling. Not a bad thing to lose in Vietnam, I decide. A funny, sour book. Not bad at all.

ABOUT THE AUTHOR

MORLEY SAFER was born in Toronto in 1931. He worked for a number of Canadian and British publications and the Canadian Broadcasting Corporation before joining CBS News as a foreign correspondent in 1964. He became coeditor of *60 Minutes* in 1970. He lives in New York City and eastern Connecticut with his wife, his daughter, and a dog named Goldie.